CAPITAL
AND ITS STRUCTURE

Studies in Economic Theory, Laurence S. Moss, Series Consultant

Economics as a Coordination Problem: *The Contributions of Friedrich A. Hayek* by Gerald P. O'Driscoll, Jr. (1977)

Liberalism: *A Socio-economic Exposition* by Ludwig von Mises (1978)

America's Great Depression, by Murray N. Rothbard (1975)

The Economic Point of View: *An Essay in the History of Economic Thought* by Israel M. Kirzner (1976)

The Foundations of Modern Austrian Economics edited with an introduction by Edwin G. Dolan (1976)

Man, Economy, and State: *A Treatise on Economic Principles* by Murray N. Rothbard (1978)

Capital, Interest, and Rent: *Essays in the Theory of Distribution* by Frank A. Fetter, edited with an introduction by Murray N. Rothbard (1977)

New Directions in Austrian Economics edited with an introduction by Louis M. Spadaro (1978)

Capital, Expectations, and the Market Process: *Essays on the Theory of the Market Economy* by Ludwig M. Lachmann, edited with an introduction by Walter E. Grinder (1977)

The Economics of Ludwig von Mises: *Toward a Critical Reappraisal* edited with an introduction by Laurence S. Moss (1976)

The Ultimate Foundation of Economic Science: *An Essay on Method* by Ludwig von Mises, with a foreword by Israel M. Kirzner (1978)

CAPITAL
AND ITS STRUCTURE

BY

LUDWIG M. LACHMANN

SHEED ANDREWS AND McMEEL, INC.
SUBSIDIARY OF UNIVERSAL PRESS SYNDICATE
KANSAS CITY

To M. L.

This edition is published in cooperation with the programs of the Institute for Humane Studies, Inc., Menlo Park, California; and Cato Institute, San Francisco, California.

Capital and Its Structure Copyright © 1978 by the Institute for Humane Studies.

The original edition of *Capital and Its Structure* was published by Bell & Sons, Ltd., on behalf of the London School of Economics and Political Science in 1956.

Library of Congress Cataloging in Publication Data

Lachmann, Ludwig M.
    Capital and its structure.

    (Studies in economic theory)
    Includes bibliographical references and index.
    1. Capital. I. Title. II. Series.
HB501.L223 1978   332'.041   77-82807
ISBN 0-8362-0740-8
ISBN 0-8362-0741-6 pbk.

Lachmann, Ludwig M

CONTENTS

CHAP.   page

PREFACE TO THE SECOND EDITION   vii

PREFACE   xiii

I   THE ORDER OF CAPITAL   1

II   ON EXPECTATIONS   20

III PROCESS ANALYSIS AND CAPITAL THEORY   35

IV   THE MEANING OF CAPITAL STRUCTURE   53

V   CAPITAL STRUCTURE AND ECONOMIC PROGRESS   72

VI   CAPITAL STRUCTURE AND ASSET STRUCTURE   86

VII CAPITAL IN THE TRADE CYCLE   100

     INDEX   129

PREFACE TO THE SECOND EDITION

An author who, after twenty years of rather heated controversy in what has come to be known as "capital theory," has a book on capital published unrevised owes his readers a word of explanation.

My first reason is that the problems constituting the subject matter of this book have little to do with what has been going on in the arena of recent controversy. This book deals with the stock of social capital and its structure, not with income accruing to the various classes of its owners. Its main concern, in Professor Hayek's formulation of thirty-six years ago, "will be to discuss in general terms what type of equipment it will be most profitable to create under various conditions, and how the equipment existing at any moment will be used, rather than to explain the factors which determined the value of a given stock of productive equipment and of the income that will be derived from it."[1] Professor Solow in 1963 assigned to capital theory an almost exactly opposite task. "In short, we really want a theory of interest rates, not a theory of capital."[2] It may be useful, then, to distinguish between Hayekian *theory of capital* and Solovian *capital theory*. This book belongs in the former category and is unaffected by the vicissitudes the latter has suffered.

The theory of capital, alas, has made little progress since 1941. This book was written about a dozen years later in an attempt to make economists aware of the existence and urgency of these structural problems. It went out of print fairly soon and was not reprinted.

My second reason for having it reprinted unchanged stems from the fact that it was written in an epoch of economic thought which now appears to be past, the era of unchallenged neoclassical ascendancy. But the neoclassical style of thought does not lend itself readily to a discussion of problems of capital structure. The

---

[1] F. A. Hayek, *Pure Theory of Capital* (London, 1941), p. 3.

[2] R. M. Solow, *Capital Theory and the Rate of Return* (Amsterdam, 1963,) p. 16.

book had to be written in a somewhat unorthodox fashion. To revise it now would be like putting steel windows in a baroque building.

In 1956 when the book first appeared, the fortunes of Austrian economics were at a low ebb. Most economists were more interested in econometrics than in subjectivism. Nobody reminded them in those days that the present, in which we stand and judge, is but a thin veneer between an unknowable future and an irrevocable past, from which our knowledge is drawn. Today this is common cause, but some of its methodological implications are as yet not well understood. The 1950s were a bad time for subjectivists. The role of expectations in economic theory, except for Shackle's pioneering efforts, was hardly appreciated. To some extent the book was a gesture of defiance to the spirit of the age. In the preface I wrote, "Our own approach in this book follows another trend of modern economic thought, not towards the 'objective' and quantifiable, but towards the subjective interpretation of phenomena." I had to review the existing theory of capital from such a perspective.

For some time one particular feature of Austrian economics had puzzled me. Its theory of capital, an essential and perhaps its best known ingredient, did not appear to fit the canon of methodological individualism. Austrians in general accepted that we must start with the individual and proceed by exploring the, often unintended, consequences of its maximizing endeavors. The Austrian theory of capital, on the other hand, from Böhm-Bawerk onward, proceeded along altogether different lines and offered little scope for the effects of individual action.

It was easy to see that this fact had something to do with Böhm-Bawerk's cast of mind. As much a Ricardian as an Austrian, he asked the old Ricardian question, how it is possible in a competitive market economy for the owners of augmentable capital resources to enjoy a permanent income. It was only in the pursuit of this endeavor that, as a means to his end, he came to construct the rudiments of a theory of capital structure. No wonder, then, that his theory looked so "objectivist" and Ricardian. It seemed to me that the most urgent task was to infuse a dose of subjectivism into this theory of capital and to relate capital phenomena to individual choices.

It is, of course, true that the "average period of production" reflects the collective time preferences of saver-consumers, but this expression in itself denotes a macroeconomic entity. Moreover, it is measurable only in a classical one-commodity world in which labor is the only factor of production, and we do not live in such a world. In a multicommodity world, on the other hand, the stock of capital is heterogeneous, and we face the task of explaining its composition in terms of individual choice.

It seemed to me that to this end the macroaggregate "capital stock" had to be broken up into smaller entities responsive to microeconomic forces, entities which can be shown to be the results, however indirect, of individual acts of choice. A theory of capital of the type envisaged had to start with the capital combinations of the individual units of production, or "firms," combinations of buildings, equipment, machines, stocks of working capital, and so forth. In them we find the "natural elements," the microeconomic roots, of the social capital stock. Within the limits set by technology, each such combination reflects the production plan of its owners and managers. It is certainly not a mere replica of the other combinations in the same "industry." The divergence of expectations makes for some variety. With product differentiation, the scope for variety is even further enhanced. One of the tasks of a theory of capital devoted to pursuing the implications of the heterogeneity and complementarity of nonpermanent resources is to explain why, even in the most fiercely competitive market, each firm bears the mark of the individuality of its leading minds.

It is to be hoped that the approach to capital followed in this book will find further development in the near future. For this, the climate may be more favorable today than it was twenty-one years ago, since our age of permanent inflation has lent urgency to some problems formerly unduly neglected. In this connection, those of capital replacement and malinvestment call for particular attention.

There was a time when most economists took the maintenance, granted. Failure in this respect would soon drive firms out of repair, and replacement of the existing capital stock very much for business. Only the bankrupt or near-bankrupt would thus fail to replace their capital resources. In any economy in which capital was normally accumulated every year, we could be sure that its existing capital stock would be duly replaced. The neoclassical notion of "steady growth" evidently rests on this assumption.

Today we have learned to be more skeptical. We now realize that capital replacement, far from being a matter of business routine, is a most problematic activity. It must rest on expectations, subjective and individual, about future income streams and choice among them. There can be no such thing as a "correct" method of depreciation and replacement in a changing world. The possibility of capital erosion in some sectors of the economy at the same time as accumulation is occurring in others is no longer to be dismissed.

That malinvestment and its consequences should have been ignored as long as macroeconomic thinking was dominated by an income-expenditure model, which had no place for capital gains and losses, is perhaps understandable, if not pardonable. It is important to realize, however, that the effects of malinvestment are not confined to the losses of wealth suffered by the capital owners directly concerned and their creditors, but that through the network of structural complementarity they may extend throughout the economic system. The appearance of malinvestment in any kind of capital resource will affect the processes of its maintenance and replacement and thus the output of its means of production, and possibly also maintenance and replacement of the latter in turn.

In our world of permanent inflation many of these problems have come to the fore. Everybody knows that in an inflation the more heavily in debt a firm is, the more profitable it appears to be, because by ordinary accounting rules the capital gains its owners make at the expense of their creditors must appear as profits. Most economists by now know this to be only an extreme case of the ubiquitous difficulty of ascertaining "true profits." But the implications of this set of problems are often not well understood.

Most contemporaries know the plight of industries with prices controlled by public authorities, usually in such a fashion that in any particular round of inflation their prices are the last to rise, but the implications for capital replacement and its repercussions mentioned earlier are less readily appreciated. In a world in which what Hicks has called "fixprices" and "flexprices" exist side by side, all industries whose output prices belong to the former, while the major portion of their input prices are of the latter category, are in approximately the same position as industries with controlled output prices.

As it is by no means obvious where current replacement cost information can be obtained, it will not help us to blame the accountants for the apparently irrational character of their rules for the evaluation of profits. These rules, on the other hand, display a tendency to turn into business institutions which decision makers dare not ignore, even where they fully understand the real issues at stake. Moreover, as Solomon Fabricant reminded us,

> the situation with regard to plant and other structures is still more difficult. Construction data assembled from a variety of sources and published in the *Survey of Current Business,* for example, are of mixed quality. Some relate to the cost of the finished structure—the building—but most relate only to the cost of materials and labor used in construction, with little or no allowance for other inputs or for productivity changes.[3]

The replacement of capital is indeed an economic activity of somewhat problematical character.

The world around us abounds with problems to which a structural theory of capital of the type outlined in this book is germane. It is to be hoped that a number of them will attract the attention of economists.

New York University
January 1977

L. M. LACHMANN

---

[3]Solomon Fabricant, "Towards Rational Accounting, in an Era of Unstable Money, 1936-1976," *National Bureau of Economic Research,* Report 16 (December 1976), p. 13.

PREFACE

For a long time now the theory of capital has been under a cloud. Twenty years ago, when Professor Knight launched his attack on the capital theories of Boehm-Bawerk and Wicksell, there opened a controversy which continued for years on both sides of the Atlantic. Today very little is heard of all this. The centre of interest has shifted to other fields.

In practice of course problems concerning capital have by no means lost their interest. There can be few economists who do not use the word 'capital' almost every day of their working lives. But apart from some notable exceptions, economists have ceased to ask fundamental questions about capital. It is pertinent to enquire why this has happened. It would seem that there are three major reasons to account for this curious neglect.

In the first place, many economists have evidently come to believe that we do not require the conceptual framework of a theory of capital in order to discuss problems germane to capital, or at least those problems in which practical interest has of late been greatest, such as investment. In other words, the view appears to have gained ground that a theory of capital is not really necessary. This, as I shall attempt to show in this book, is an erroneous view. It is hardly possible to discuss the causes and consequences of a change in a stock without some knowledge of the nature and composition of this stock; or, it is only possible to do so if we are prepared to abstract from all those features of the situation which really matter. In the discussion of capital problems, as of any other problems, we cannot dispense with a coherent frame of reference.

A second reason for the present-day neglect of the theory of capital has probably to be sought in the contemporary preoccupation with quantitative precision of statement and argument. Most contemporary economics is presented in a quantitative garb. This is not the place to enquire into the reasons for this predilection. To some extent of course economists, in spending so much effort on quantifying the terms in which they present their theories, wittingly or unwittingly merely reflect the spirit of our age.

But why should such quantification be more problematical in the theory of capital than it is in other fields of economic study? In most business transactions capital is treated as a quantity. In every balance sheet we find a capital account.

The fact remains, however, that in spite of protracted efforts it has proved impossible to find a quantitative expression for capital which would satisfy the rigorous requirements of economic thought. Most economists agree today that, except under equilibrium conditions, a 'quantity of capital' is not a meaningful concept. In this book an attempt is made to follow up some implications of this conclusion. But the fact that the concept of capital has for so long proved refractory to all attempts at quantification is almost certainly one of the reasons for the lack of interest, and hence of progress, in the theory of capital.

A third reason, closely related to the one just mentioned, appears to lie in the rather peculiar nature of the relationship between capital and knowledge. The various uses made of any durable capital good reflect the accumulated experience and knowledge gained, in workshop and market, by those who operate it. But modern economic theory cannot easily cope with change that is not quantitative change; and knowledge is as refractory to quantification as capital is. The acquisition and diffusion of knowledge certainly take place in time, but neither is, in any meaningful sense of the word, a 'function' of time. Modern economists, uneasily aware of the problem, have tried to avoid it by assuming a 'given state of knowledge'. But such an assumption, if taken literally, would obviously prevent us from considering economic change of any kind. For instance, as Mrs. Robinson has pointed out, 'a "change in methods of production in a given state of knowledge" is, strictly speaking, a contradiction in terms'. With very durable capital goods the assumption becomes quite untenable. Our railways after all are not run by people with the technical knowledge of 125 years ago.

The theory of capital is a dynamic theory, not merely because many capital goods are durable, but because the changes in use which these durable capital goods undergo during their life-time reflect the acquisition and transmission of knowledge.

Our own approach in this book follows another trend of modern economic thought, not towards the 'objective' and quantifiable, but towards the subjective interpretation of phenomena. Of late many economists have exercised their ingenuity in fashioning their science in accordance with the rigid canons of Logical Empiricism. Even the theory of value has been made to conform to the strict rules of the behaviourists: nowadays we are not supposed to know anything about human preferences until these have been 'revealed' to us. But few of these efforts have been successful. The fact remains that the two greatest achievements of our science within the last hundred years, subjective value and the introduction of expectations, became possible only when it was realized that the causes of certain phenomena do not lie in the 'facts of the situation' but in the appraisal of such a situation by active minds.

The generic concept of capital without which economists cannot do their work has no measurable counterpart among material objects; it reflects the entrepreneurial appraisal of such objects. Beer barrels and blast furnaces, harbour installations and hotel-room furniture are capital not by virtue of their physical properties but by virtue of their economic functions. Something is capital because the market, the consensus of entrepreneurial minds, regards it as capable of yielding an income. This does not mean that the phenomena of capital cannot be comprehended by clear and unambiguous concepts. The stock of capital used by society does not present a picture of chaos. Its arrangement is not arbitrary. There is some order in it. This book is devoted to the exploration of the problems of the order of capital.

The chief object of this book is thus to rekindle interest in the fundamental problems of capital rather than to present a closed system of generalizations about them; to outline a new approach and to show that it can be applied, with some promise of success, to a number of such problems ranging from the productivity of capital to the demise of the 'strong boom'; to point out the implications of certain economic facts which have been long neglected; and, above all, to emphasize the transmission of knowledge, the interaction of minds, as the ultimate agent of all economic processes.

I am painfully aware of the fact that this book leaves many vital questions unanswered. It could hardly be otherwise. But it is my hope that others will follow and make their contributions to the theory of capital. There can be few fields of economic enquiry today which promise a richer harvest than the systematic study of the modes of use of our material resources.

It is not impossible that at some time in the future the concept of capital structure, the order in which the various capital resources are arranged in the economic system, will be given a quantitative expression; after all, any order can be expressed in numbers. For many reasons such a development would be most welcome. But this book has been written to meet the present situation in which we badly need a generic concept of capital, but in which all attempts to express it in quantitative terms have thus far been unsuccessful.

My greatest debt of gratitude is to Professor F. A. Hayek whose ideas on capital have helped to shape my own thought more than those of any other thinker. To Professor F. W. Paish who, during his stay at this University in 1952 as a Visiting Trust Fund Lecturer, undaunted by a heavily loaded time-table, read several chapters in draft form, I am indebted for much sagacious comment and advice. In writing the final version of Chapter VI I have drawn heavily on his unrivalled knowledge of the intricacies of modern business finance. But needless to say, the responsibility for what I say is entirely mine.

I owe more than I can express in words to my friends in the University of the Witwatersrand for their steady help and encouragement, in particular to Mr. L. H. Samuels and Mr. T. van Waasdijk, who patiently read draft after draft, and from whose helpful comment and suggestions I have derived much unearned profit.

I also wish to express my gratitude to the Research Committee of this University who by their generous financial assistance have considerably eased my task.

Lastly, I have to thank the Royal Economic Society, the editor and publishers of the *Manchester School of Economic and*

Social Studies, Messrs. George Allen & Unwin, the McGraw-Hill Book Company, Inc., and Messrs. Routledge & Kegan Paul for permission to quote passages from works published by them. I also wish to acknowledge my gratitude to the authors of these passages.

L. M. LACHMANN

University of the Witwatersrand
  Johannesburg
    September, 1955

CHAPTER I

THE ORDER OF CAPITAL

The realm of economics consists of many provinces between which, in the course of time, a fairly high degree of inter-regional division of labour has evolved. Naturally, development in some of these regions has been faster than in others. There are some 'backward areas', and a few of them actually appear to merit description as 'distressed areas'. None seems to have a better claim to this unenviable status than the Theory of Capital. In fact it would hardly be an exaggeration to say that at the present time a systematic theory of capital scarcely exists.

Considering the degree of division of labour just mentioned this surely is an astonishing state of affairs. There can hardly be a field of economic thought, pure or applied, in which the word 'capital' is not more or less constantly employed. We hear of a world-wide capital shortage. In discussions on the convertibility of currencies we are asked to distinguish between 'current' and capital transactions. And it is clear that the 'economic integration of Western Europe' requires that some at least of the industrial resources of these countries be re-grouped and change their form; in other words, that it entails a modification of Europe's capital structure.

Yet, in the Theory of Capital the present state of affairs is as we have described it. The product imported and used by the other economic disciplines is not a standardized product. The word 'capital', as used by economists, has no clear and unambiguous meaning. Sometimes the word denotes the material resources of production, sometimes their money value. Sometimes it means money sums available for loan or the purchase of assets. While to some economists 'capital' has come to mean nothing but the present value of future income streams. The conclusion suggests itself that no progress made in the theory of capital could fail to pay handsome dividends in the form of 'external economies' to be reaped by all those who have to work with the notion of capital.

1

The root of the trouble is well known: *capital resources are heterogeneous.* Capital, as distinct from labour and land, lacks a 'natural' unit of measurement. While we may add head to head (even woman's head to man's head) and acre to acre (possibly weighted by an index of fertility) we cannot add beer barrels to blast furnaces nor trucks to yards of telephone wire. Yet, the economist cannot do his work properly without a generic concept of capital. Where he has to deal with quantitative change he needs a common denominator. Almost inevitably he follows the business man in adopting money value as his standard of measurement of capital change. This means that whenever relative money values change, we lose our common denominator.

In equilibrium, where, by definition, all values are consistent with each other, the use of money value as a unit of measurement is not necessarily an illegitimate procedure.[1] But in disequilibrium where no such consistency exists, it cannot be applied. The dilemma has been known ever since Wicksell drew attention to it.[2] But in most current discussions on capital the whole problem with its manifold implications, which go far beyond the confines of the theory of capital, is, as a rule, allowed to be ignored.

In confronting this dilemma it seems best to start by setting forth a few fundamental facts about capital.

All capital resources are heterogeneous. The heterogeneity which matters is here, of course, not physical heterogeneity, but heterogeneity in use. Even if, at some future date, some miraculous substance were invented, a very light metal perhaps, which it was found profitable to substitute for all steel, wood, copper, etc., so that all capital equipment were to be made from it, this would in no way affect our problem. The real economic significance of the heterogeneity of capital lies in the fact that each capital good can only be used for a limited number of purposes. We shall speak of the *multiple specificity* of capital goods.

---

[1] 'But although, even in the analysis of a stationary equilibrium, the inclusion of the "quantity of capital" among the determinants of that equilibrium means that something which is the result of the equilibrating process, is treated as if it were a datum, this confusion was made relatively innocuous by the essential limitations of the static method, which while it describes the conditions of a state of equilibrium, does not explain how such a state is brought about.' F. A. von Hayek: *Profits, Interest and Investment*, pp. 83–4.
[2] *Lectures on Political Economy*, Vol. I, p. 202.

Each capital good is, at every moment, devoted to what in the circumstances appears to its owner to be its 'best', i.e. its most profitable use. The word 'best' indicates a position on a scale of alternative possibilities. Changing circumstances will change that position. Unexpected change may open up new possibilities of use, and make possible a switch from yesterday's 'best' to an even better use. Or, it may compel a switch from 'present best' to 'second best' use. Hence, we cannot be surprised to find that at each moment some durable capital goods are not being used for the purposes for which they were originally designed. These new uses may, from the point of view of the owners of the capital goods, be 'better' or 'worse', more or less profitable than the original ones. In each case the change in use means that the original plan in which the capital good was meant to play its part has gone astray. In most of the arguments about capital encountered today these facts and their implications, many of them crucial to a clear understanding of the nature of economic progress, are almost completely ignored.

It is hard to imagine any capital resource which by itself, operated by human labour but without the use of other capital resources, could turn out any output at all. For most purposes capital goods have to be used jointly. *Complementarity* is of the essence of capital use. But the heterogeneous capital resources do not lend themselves to combination in any arbitrary fashion. For any given number of them only certain modes of complementarity are technically possible, and only a few of these are economically significant. It is among the latter that the entrepreneur has to find the 'optimum combination'. The 'best' mode of complementarity is thus not a 'datum'. It is in no way 'given' to the entrepreneur who, on the contrary, as a rule has to spend a good deal of time and effort in finding out what it is. Even where he succeeds quickly he will not enjoy his achievement for long, as sooner or later circumstances will begin to change again.

Unexpected change, whenever it occurs, will make possible, or compel, changes in the use of capital goods. It will thus cause the disintegration of existing capital combinations. Even where it opens up new and promising possibilities for some resources it will open them up for some, not for all. The rest will have to be turned to second-best uses. It is because of these facts that it is impossible to measure capital. Capital has no 'natural' measure, and value will be affected by every unexpected change.

Yet, we need a generic concept. We want to be able to speak of 'Capital'. Logically, we can establish no systematic generalization without a generic concept. But we need more than that. Unable as we are to measure capital resources, we must at least make an attempt to classify them. If there can be no common denominator there should at least be a *criterium ordinis*. The stock of capital does not present a picture of chaos; its arrangement is not arbitrary; there is some order in it. As we saw, capital resources cannot be combined in an arbitrary fashion. Only some modes of complementarity are economically significant. These form the basis of the capital order.

If our classification of capital resources is to be realistic, the criterion of order we employ must correspond to the order in which these resources are in reality arranged. As all capital resources exist for the sake of the uses to which they are, or may be, put, this means that we must make our conceptual order reflect the actual pattern of capital use. The elements of this pattern are the capital combinations of the various enterprises, and they in their totality form the *capital structure* of society. Entrepreneurial decisions on capital combinations are the immediate determinants of the Order of Capital, though, on a wider view, these decisions reflect, of course, the complex interaction of economic forces from which the entrepreneur takes his orientation. It will be our main task in this book to study the changes which this network of capital relationships, within firms and between firms, undergoes as the result of unexpected change. To this end we must regard the 'stock of capital' not as a homogeneous aggregate but as a structural pattern. The Theory of Capital is, in the last resort, the morphology of the forms which this pattern assumes in a changing world.

We may turn aside for a moment to consider how economists in the past have coped with the problem of the capital order.

The classical economists, when they spoke of the 'stock of

capital', conceived of it as homogeneous and measurable, like any other stock. From Ricardo onwards, of course, their main interest was in the distribution of incomes. Capital was of importance mainly as the 'source' of profit in the same way as labour was the source of wages and land the source of rent. And as the rate of profit was regarded as tending towards equality in all uses of capital, the problem was really posed only under equilibrium conditions. For only here is there a determinate and homogeneous quantity which we may call 'output', and as profit is conceived as part of homogeneous output, so its 'source' would appear to be equally homogeneous.

The notion of a homogeneous capital stock no doubt was borrowed, as are so many of our concepts, from accounting practice which makes a (homogeneous) money sum appear in the capital account. Now, the classical economists were certainly not unaware of some of the dangers of describing economic magnitudes in money terms. But in this case the danger seemed to be avoided, and the notion of a 'real stock' gained a certain plausibility from the employment of two devices which played a prominent part in the classical doctrine. On the one hand, the labour theory of value made it possible and necessary to reduce capital values to labour values, i.e. to homogeneous labour units. On the other hand, there was the concept of the Wages Fund which not merely served to render the stock of capital homogeneous but also reduced all capital goods to consumption goods measurable in labour units.

In the neo-classical schools which rose in the last three decades of the last century the focus of interest is still distribution, explained now by the marginal productivity principle. Here factors of production of various classes between which there is no longer over-all homogeneity, though the members of each class are still regarded as homogeneous, produce a homogeneous product. The Wages Fund is abandoned, but the new problem which emerges now that capital goods can no longer be regarded as consumption goods *in statu nascendi*, viz. the effect of capital change on capital values in terms of consumable output, is ignored.

The analysis is still couched in equilibrium terms. But capital is no longer measured in labour, or any other cost, units, and 'no one ever makes it clear how capital is to be

B

measured'.[3] Reasoning based on the marginal productivity principle can no longer be applied to capital even where the change is, within the framework of 'comparative statics', from one equilibrium to another. *A fortiori* it is impossible to speak of capital in quantitative terms in conditions of disequilibrium.

More recently the focus of interest in discussions on capital has shifted to Investment, defined as the 'net addition to the capital stock'. Now, it is possible to define the economic forces engendering investment in terms which avoid the quantification of capital, or even the very concept of capital. Professor Lerner, for instance, has defined his 'marginal efficiency of investment' exclusively in terms of present output forgone and future output obtained.[4] But in any realistic discussion of the 'inducement to invest' it is clearly impossible to ignore existing capital resources, on the use and profitability of which the new capital cannot but have some effect.

A theory of investment based on the assumption of a homogeneous and quantifiable capital stock is bound to ignore important features of reality. Owing to its very character it can only deal with quantitative capital change, investment and disinvestment. It cannot deal with *changes in the composition of the stock*. Yet there can be little doubt that such changes in the composition of the stock are of fundamental importance in many respects, but in particular with regard to the causes and effects of investment. As long as we cling to the view that all capital is homogeneous, we shall only see, as Keynes did, the unfavourable effects of investment on the earning capacity and value of existing capital goods, since all the elements of a homogeneous aggregate are necessarily perfect substitutes for each other. The new capital competes with the old and reduces the profitability of the latter. Once we allow for heterogeneity we must also allow for complementarity between old and new capital. The effect of investment on the profitability of old capital is now seen to depend on which of the various forms of old capital are complementary to, or substitutes for, the new capital. The effect on the complements

[3] Joan Robinson: *The Rate of Interest, and other Essays*, p. 54.
[4] A. P. Lerner: 'On the Marginal Product of Capital and the Marginal Efficiency of Investment', *Journal of Political Economy*, February 1953, see especially pp. 6–9.

will be favourable, on the substitutes unfavourable. The 'inducement to invest' will therefore often depend on the effect the new capital is expected to have on the earning capacity of old capital complementary to it. In other words, investment decisions, as to their magnitude, and even more as to the concrete form they are likely to take, depend at each moment on the prevailing composition of the existing capital stock. In general, investments will tend to take such concrete forms as are complementary to the capital already in existence. A real understanding of the investment pattern is therefore impossible as long as we cling to the homogeneity hypothesis. Investment is thus seen to be ultimately a problem of the capital order. At each moment it reflects, both as regards its quantitative volume and its concrete form, the possibilities left open by the existing capital order.

We must now return to our main task in this chapter. We shall attempt to present very briefly a preliminary view of the chief problems with which we shall be concerned in this book. The problem of capital as a 'source' of profit is not among them. In Chapter V, to be sure, we shall have occasion to examine certain aspects of the theory of interest, but in the context of this book this will be to us a mere side-line. The main subject-matter of this book is *the Capital Structure*. When we turn our attention to the relationship between capital and interest we do it for the light that interest sheds on capital, not vice versa. Those economists to whom the concept of capital was in the main an instrument in their search for the explanation of the interest phenomenon naturally conceived of it as a homogeneous aggregate consisting of value units. By contrast, our conception of capital is that of a complex structure which is *functionally differentiated* in that the various capital resources of which it is composed have different functions. The allocation of these functions, and the changes which its mode undergoes in a world of change, is one of our main problems.

In this book we shall endeavour to outline an approach to capital problems which is both realistic and directly based on the definition of economic action: realistic in that we deal with the world of unexpected change; directly based on the definition of economic action in that we start from the fact that capital resources are scarce resources *with alternative uses.*[5] To us the chief problem of the theory of capital is to explain why capital resources are used in the way they are; why in a given situation some alternatives are rejected, others selected; what governs the choice or rejection of alternative uses when unexpected change compels a revision of plan. There are two broad answers to these questions, the first of which is perhaps rather trite, but the second of which has not as yet been given the prominent place it deserves in economic thought. The first answer is that, of course, capital goods must be used in such a way as to produce, directly or indirectly, the goods and services consumers want at prices they are prepared to pay. This is a familiar theme. The urge to maximize profits warrants the belief that after some trial and error capital goods will in reality be used in such a fashion. But there is a second answer. Capital uses must 'fit into each other'. Each capital good has a function which forms part of a plan. Capital goods with no such function will not be maintained. The fact that capital goods which do not 'earn their keep' will be discarded warrants the belief that a tendency towards the integration of the capital structure really exists. But while, on the one hand, the scope of this phenomenon is wider than is commonly recognized, the tendency does not operate unimpeded.

It is obvious that capital equipment for which no labour can be found to work it, is useless and will be scrapped. Once we abandon the assumption that all capital is homogeneous the scope of this phenomenon is seen to extend beyond that of the complementarity between labour and capital. Capital equipment may have to be scrapped because no capital combination can be found into which it would fit.

On the other hand, the scrapping of surplus capital, and consequently the integration of the capital structure, may in reality be delayed for a number of reasons. For one thing, expectations of a future different from the present may spoil the simplicity of our theorem. If capital owners think that

[5] We do not wish to imply, of course, that other capital theories are not based on, or do not conform to, the definition of economic action and the praxeological axioms it entails. But all too often the link is rather tenuous.

There is a 'missing link' in most equilibrium theories; they all have to assume that, once the data are given, the problem of how equilibrium is reached has been solved. By contrast we shall concern ourselves with the 'path' which men have to follow in building up capital combinations and using them.

complementary factors will be available in the future, they will prefer to wait. Moreover, for heavy durable equipment the annual cost of maintenance is probably relatively small. This means that even a small profit may suffice to keep capital goods in existence. Owners of displaced capital goods will then try to find complementary resources by offering their owners co-operation on favourable terms. This, of course, is what we meant by 'switching capital goods to second-best use'. Before displaced capital goods are scrapped attempts will thus be made to lure other capital goods, potentially complements to them, out of the combinations of which they happen to form part. To some extent these attempts will be successful. This is important as it gives rise to certain dynamic processes we shall study in Chapter III. As we shall see, equilibrium analysis cannot be applied to them.

For the present we may conclude that a tendency towards the integration of the capital structure exists, but that it may encounter resistance from optimistic expectations and the possibility of multiple use. While the former will lead to 'surplus stocks' and the maintenance of other forms of visible excess capacity which have of late attracted the attention of economists, the latter will give rise to a kind of invisible excess capacity, a counterpart to 'disguised unemployment'. Capital resources will be used in ways for which they were not planned, but these uses will be discontinued the moment complementary resources make their appearance.

It is evident that only a morphological theory can be expected to cope with such problems. Whether in reality an integrated capital structure, in the sense that every capital good has a function, can exist in a world of unexpected change remains to be seen. But we may say that the desire to maximize profits on existing capital goods and the obvious futility of maintaining those that cannot, either now or in the fore-seeable future, be fitted into the existing structure, warrant the belief that economic action will at each moment tend in the direction of such an integrated structure, even though this may never be completed.

All this has implications for the theory of investment. We cannot explain how either existing resources are being replaced, whether by their replicas or otherwise, or what kind of new

capital goods is being created, without having first of all learnt
how existing capital is being used.   The shape in which new
capital goods make their appearance is determined largely by
the existing pattern, in the sense that 'investment opportunities'
really mean 'holes in the pattern'.

In the traditional view, maintained by Keynes and his
followers, new investment follows the success of similar existing
capital combinations.   If shipping lines have been profitable
more ships will be built.   While, to be sure, the marginal
efficiency of capital is defined as an expectational magnitude,
we are always given to understand that high profits on existing
capital offer a strong incentive to invest while low profits do
not.   As we shall see, this is another illegitimate generalization
based on the homogeneity hypothesis.   A number of investment opportunities actually owe their existence to the failure
of past capital combinations to achieve the purposes for which
they were designed.   This problem will be discussed also in
Chapter III.

All capital goods have to fit into a pattern or structure.
What determines the structure?   In the first place, there are
the various production plans, which determine the use to which
each capital good will be put.   But if we are to speak of a
structure, these plans must be consistent with each other.
What makes them so?   The market compels the readjustment
of those production plans which are inconsistent with either
consumers' plans or other production plans.   From the push
and pull of market forces there emerges finally a network of
plans which determines the pattern of capital use.

But the economic forces which integrate the capital structure
via the network of plans should not be confused with the force,
discussed above, which causes the re-integration of the structure
by discarding surplus equipment.   The former serve to
minimize, though they cannot altogether eliminate, the impact
of unexpected change by removing inconsistency of plans.
The latter only comes into operation after unexpected change
has happened and caused some capital to be displaced.   The
former will be discussed at some length in Chapter IV.

We hope to have persuaded the reader that once we abandon
the homogeneity hypothesis we are compelled to adopt a
morphological approach to the problems of capital, which

must supersede purely quantitative reasoning. For the quantitative concept of a homogeneous stock we have to substitute the concept of a functionally differentiated Capital Structure.[6]

As yet we have left the concept of Capital undefined. We now define it as the (heterogeneous) *stock of material resources*. In thus defining it we follow Walras in stressing heterogeneity ('les capitaux proprement dits') and Irving Fisher in refusing to draw the traditional distinction between land and capital. In fact, all the three possible criteria of distinction between land and other material resources are readily seen to be irrelevant to our purpose.

When capital is defined, with Boehm-Bawerk, as the 'produced means of production' land is, of course, excluded. But to us the question which matters is not which resources are man-made but which are man-used. Historical origin is no concern of ours. Our interest lies in the uses to which a resource is put. In this respect land is no different from other resources. Every capital combination is in fact a combination of land and other resources. Changes in the composition of such combinations are of just as much interest to us where land is, as where it is not affected.

A second criterion of distinction between land and other capital resources is based on the contrast between the 'fixed' nature of the supply of land and the variable character of the supply of other material resources. The criterion is quantitative in a purely physical sense which is not necessarily economically relevant. There are even today large tracts of undeveloped land in the world which could be brought into productive use by combining them with capital resources. In other words, there is 'physical' land which is not a source of economic services. The conditions in which such economic transformation will take place are precisely a problem in the theory of capital. To ignore them is to ignore one of the most significant dynamic aspects of capital.

[6] Professor S. Herbert Frankel has for some time expounded a similar view. 'Capital . . . is, apart from the symbolism of accounting, always "concrete" in the sense that it is embedded in, and attuned to, the particular purposes and state of knowledge which led to its "creation". It is but temporarily incorporated in ever changing forms and patterns suited to the evanescent ends for which it is designed' (*The Economic Impact on Under-developed Societies*, 1953, p. 69).

Professor Hayek has defined capital as 'those non-permanent resources which can be used only . . . to contribute to the *permanent* maintenance of the income at a particular level'.[7] Permanent resources thus fall outside the scope of this definition and outside the scope of the theory of capital. But we cannot adopt this definition as we cannot ignore the uses to which permanent resources are put. There is no reason to believe that in their case the pattern of resource use is fundamentally different from that of non-permanent resources. In fact, as we said above, the two are almost invariably used together. This does not mean that the replacement, the recurrent need for which is the distinguishing characteristic of non-permanent resources, is of no interest to us. In so far as replacement does not take the form of the production of mere replicas it is of interest to us as it changes the composition of the capital stock. But what distinguishes our approach from Professor Hayek's is that we are not concerned with the maintenance of income at a particular level. We are not interested in that long period which must elapse before the income-stream from non-permanent resources dries up, but in the series of short periods during which resources are shifted from one use to another, and in the repercussions of such shifts. The causes and repercussions of these shifts are more or less the same, whether the resources shifted are permanent or not (except for very short-lived resources). As long as the period during which income-streams from non-permanent resources might be exhausted remains beyond our horizon, there is no reason why we should distinguish between permanent and non-permanent resources. The growing predominance of very durable capital equipment in modern industrial society appears to underline the pointlessness of the distinction and justify our neglect of it.

We shall now briefly set out the logical structure of the argument thus far presented in this chapter.

Heterogeneity of Capital means heterogeneity in use;
Heterogeneity in use implies Multiple Specificity;
Multiple Specificity implies Complementarity;
Complementarity implies Capital Combinations;
Capital Combinations form the elements of *the Capital Structure.*

[7] *The Pure Theory of Capital,* p. 54.

We are living in a world of unexpected change; hence capital combinations, and with them the capital structure, will be ever changing, will be dissolved and re-formed. In this activity we find the real function of the entrepreneur.

We must now give some consideration to the method of analysis which we shall employ in this book. Multiple Specificity, as we saw, is a characteristic of the capital resources which form the subject-matter of this book. Their mode of use changes as circumstances change. Their life-story thus falls naturally into a sequence of periods during each of which we note their use for a specific purpose in conjunction with labour services and other capital goods. This fact already points to the need for Period Analysis in studying the pattern of capital use. It is not, however, a mere matter of time, but of human action in time.

The employment of a number of capital goods in a capital combination during a given period is embodied in a production plan made at the beginning of the period. The plan thus provides a scheme of orientation, a frame of reference for subsequent action. This pattern of resource use will be continued as long as the plan succeeds in the sense that a 'target' envisaged in it is attained. The method to be employed in describing such events might thus be strictly called 'Plan-Period-Analysis'. And inasmuch as we have to go beyond the 'unit period', and consider what happens in the next period as a result of what happened in this, we shall speak of Process Analysis. In the context which alone interests us this means that if the plan fails the capital combination will be dissolved and its constituent elements turned to other uses, each within the range permitted by its multiple specificity.

The method of Process Analysis has been described by Professor Lindahl in a famous passage:

> Starting from the plans and the external conditions valid at the initial point of time, we have first to deduce the development that will be the result of these data for a certain period forward during which no relevant changes in the plans are assumed to occur. Next we have to investigate how far the development during this first period—involving as it must various surprises for the economic subjects—will force them to revise their plans of action for the future, the principles for such a revision being

assumed to be included in the data of the problem. And since
on this basis the development during the second period is
determined in the same manner as before, fresh deductions
must be made concerning the plans for the third period, and
so on.[8]

In this book we shall thus employ the method of process
analysis based on plans and those entrepreneurial decisions
which accompany their success and failure. But we shall not
indulge in building 'dynamic models' based on 'behaviour
functions' expressed in terms of 'difference equations'. Our
reason for this refusal is that to assume that entrepreneurial
conduct in revising plans at the end of successive periods is, in
any objective sense, *determined* by past experience and thus
predictable, would mean falling into a rigid determinism which
is quite contrary to everyday experience.

Men in society come to learn about each other's needs and
resources and modify their conduct in accordance with such
knowledge. But the acquisition of this knowledge follows no
definite pattern, certainly no time-pattern. Knowledge is not
acquired merely as time goes by.

All human conduct is, of course, moulded by experience,
but there is a *subjective* element in the *interpretation* of experience
to ignore which would be a retrograde step. Different men
react to the same experience in different ways. Were we con-
concerned with 'Macro-dynamics' all this might not matter
very much. Probability might provide a convenient way out.
But we are concerned with the conduct of the individual entrepreneur. A rigid determinism in these matters would appear
to reflect an outmoded, pre-Knightian approach. The econo-
metricians have thus far failed to explain why in an uncertain
world the meaning of past events should be the only certain
thing, and why its 'correct' interpretation by entrepreneurs
can always be taken for granted.

To assume 'given behaviour functions' or 'entrepreneurial
reaction equations' is simply to deny that entrepreneurs are
capable of interpreting historical experience, i.e. experience
which does not repeat itself. In other words, to make these
assumptions is to say that entrepreneurs are automata and have

[8] Erik Lindahl: *Studies in the Theory of Money and Capital* (George Allen & Unwin
Ltd.), pp. 38-9.

no minds. Observation, however, bears out the contention that entrepreneurial minds exist and function.

The entrepreneurial interpretation of past experience finds its most interesting manifestation in the formation of *expectations*. Expectations, i.e. those acts of the entrepreneurial mind which constitute his 'world', diagnose 'the situation' in which action has to be taken, and logically precede the making of plans, are of crucial importance for process analysis. A method of dynamic analysis which fails to allow for variable expectations due to subjective interpretation seems bound to degenerate into a series of economically irrelevant mathematical exercises.

It thus seems clear that a study of capital problems in a world of unexpected change has to be conducted by means of process analysis, and that the application of this method presupposes a study of entrepreneurial expectations.

The plan of this book is conceived in the following manner: In Chapter II we start by establishing a few systematic generalizations about expectations. In doing so we shall have to delve much more deeply into the subject than has been the case in recent discussions. Arguments about how people bring the various possible outcomes of actions they envisage into consistency with each other will be seen to be quite inadequate for our purpose. The formation of expectations is a moment in the process of the acquisition of knowledge and has to be studied as such. In Chapter III we shall show how process analysis can be applied to capital problems; how entrepreneurs react to unexpected change by forming and dissolving capital combinations in the light of experience gained from working with them. In Chapter IV we ask how a capital structure can come to exist in a world of unexpected change. We shall see that, though in the real world a capital structure integrating all existing capital resources, even if it ever came into existence, could not exist for any length of time, integrating as well as disintegrating forces are always in operation, and much can be learned from a study of their *modus operandi*.

The Chapters II to IV constitute the theoretical nucleus of the book. In the following three chapters the ideas set forth in the earlier part will be applied to a variety of capital problems. In Chapter V we attempt to show that, in so far as the accumulation of capital can be said to prompt economic progress, it does so by prompting certain typical changes in the composition of the capital stock. In Chapter VI we raise the question whether structural relationships exist in the sphere of property rights and claims as well as in that of physical capital resources, and if so, how the two spheres are interrelated. In Chapter VII we hope to show that if capital accumulation entails changes in the composition of the capital stock, it also entails certain consequences for the course of the Trade Cycle; that industrial fluctuations are frequently due to intersectional maladjustment, and that in the circumstances which usually accompany economic progress this is often almost inevitable. Finally, some attention will be given to the question of how such maladjustments can be, and are in reality, overcome.

The argument so far set forth in this chapter, derived as it is from heterogeneity and multiple specificity of capital, has a number of implications which will come up for fuller discussion at various points in the book. But a few of them which, in a sense, underlie all that follows should be noted already now.

What we have so far said in this chapter serves to sharpen our understanding of the function of the entrepreneur. We usually say that the entrepreneur 'combines factor services'. So he does, but the statement is too wide and not precise enough since it suggests that the relationship between the entrepreneur and the owners of resources, human and material, is symmetrical in all cases. Labour, of course, is hired and dismissed. But the entrepreneur's function as regards capital is not exhausted by the hire of services. Here his function is to *specify* and make decisions on the concrete form the capital resources shall have. He specifies and modifies the shape and layout of his plant, which is something he cannot do to his typists, desirable though that may seem to him. As long as we disregard the heterogeneity of capital, the true function of the entrepreneur must also remain hidden. In a homogeneous world there is no scope for the activity of specifying.

This fact is of some practical importance. For it follows that the entrepreneur carries, and must carry, a much heavier responsibility towards the owners of his capital than towards his workers, since as regards the resources of the former he enjoys a much wider range of discretion than as regards those of the latter. It means not merely that 'workers' control of industry' is impossible. It also means that capital owners, having delegated the power of specification to the entrepreneur, are 'uncertainty-bearers' in a sense in which workers are not. They are in fact themselves entrepreneurs of a special kind. The whole relationship between manager-entrepreneurs and capitalist-entrepreneurs will be taken up for discussion towards the end of Chapter VI.

From time to time, in particular in the last three chapters of this book, we shall employ the notion of 'economic progress'. By this we mean an increase in real income per head. We must note that to assume progress is not necessarily the same thing as to assume the 'dynamic' conditions of a world of unexpected change. On the one hand, of course, dynamic conditions may lead not to progress but to disaster. On the other hand, most recent discussions of progress have been couched in terms not of a dynamic world, but of the model of an 'expanding economy', of Cassel's 'uniformly progressive economy' slightly modified by Messrs. Harrod and Hicks. This model embodies the notion of 'growth', of progress at a known and *expected* rate. Its significance for the real world, however, is doubtful. Already the metaphor 'growth' is singularly inappropriate to the real world as it suggests a process during which the harmony of proportions remains undisturbed. Nor can we, after what has been said, any longer believe that progress will manifest itself in the capital sphere merely in the form of capital accumulation, i.e. purely quantitative growth. In what follows we shall always assume that progress takes place in conditions of unexpected change.

Inevitably unexpected change entails some capital gains and losses. Hence we cannot say that progress is either accompanied or caused by the accumulation of capital. But the malinvestment of capital may, in some cases, by providing external economies, become the starting-point of a process of development. A railway line built for the exploitation of some mineral resource may be a failure, but may nevertheless give rise to more intensive forms of agriculture on land adjacent to it by providing dairy farmers with transport for their produce. Such instances play a more important part in economic progress than is commonly realized. The ability to turn failure into success and to benefit from the discomfiture of others is the crucial test of true entrepreneurship. A progressive economy is not an economy in which no capital is ever lost, but an economy which can afford to lose capital because the productive opportunities revealed by the loss are vigorously exploited. Each investment is planned for a given environment, but as a cumulative result of sustained investment activity the environment changes. These changes in environment did not appear on the horizon of any of the entrepreneurial planners at the time when the plan was conceived. All that matters is that new plans which take account of the change in environment should be made forthwith and old plans adjusted accordingly. If this is done as fast as the new knowledge becomes available there will be no hitch in the concatenation of processes, of plan and action, which we call progress.

What we have just said has some relevance to the problems of the 'economic development of underdeveloped areas' which have in recent years been so extensively discussed by economists and others.[9] Economic progress, we saw, is a process which involves trial and error. In its course new knowledge is acquired gradually, often painfully, and always at some cost to somebody.[10] In other words, some capital gains and losses are inevitable as durable capital goods, in the course of their long lives, have to be used for purposes other than those for which they were originally designed. Such capital losses have been frequent concomitants of economic progress in the history of almost all industrial countries, and have on the whole done much good and little harm.

But a question arises in this connection which has, to our knowledge, rarely been adequately discussed: Who will bear the risk? Where economic development is financed by risk

[9] In these discussions Professor Frankel has shown himself an undaunted critic of the quantitative notion of capital which most other writers on the subject accepted without question. In particular, he frequently warned his fellow-economists 'not to regard the calculations of the private entrepreneur in terms of established accounting symbolisms as in any sense an automatic or mechanical process' (S. H. Frankel, op. cit., p. 66).

[10] For examples see S. H. Frankel, op. cit., pp. 101–2.

capital, capital owners, of course, bear the risk of loss. But risk capital is now rapidly becoming very scarce everywhere in the world, even in those countries in which it is not actually being taxed out of existence. On the other hand, the political myths of the twentieth century being what they are, politicians in most underdeveloped countries abhor the very thought of foreign risk-bearing capitalists, or, if they do not, at least have to pretend before the electorate that they harbour such feelings. The reason is not far to seek: He who bears the risk must also appoint the managers. In the prevailing climate of opinion the economic development of such countries will therefore largely have to be promoted with the help of loan capital. This means that the capital losses will have to be borne by those who are probably least able to bear them, viz. the inhabitants of these areas themselves, whose rescue from poverty has been, after all, the ostensible purpose of the whole operation!

CHAPTER II

ON EXPECTATIONS

The explicit introduction of expectations into the economic theories of the last thirty years has given rise to a host of new problems. Of these the most fundamental is the question whether expectations have to be regarded as independent 'data' or as the results of economic processes. As yet, economists appear to disagree on the answer; hence the unsatisfactory state of the theory of expectations.

Evidently expectations are not economic results in the sense in which prices and output quantities are. No economic process *determines* them. A 10 per cent rise in the price of apples may just as well give rise to an expectation of a further rise as to that of a future fall. It all depends on the circumstances accompanying the rise, and different people may give these circumstances a different interpretation. It follows that all those dynamic theories which are based on 'difference equations', 'accelerators', etc., simply by-pass our problem. At best we may regard them as provisional hypotheses to be employed as long as the wider questions remain unanswered.

It is, however, equally impossible to treat expectations as *data* in the same way as we treat consumers' tastes. From whatever angle we look at them, expectations reflect economic experience and are affected by changes in it. In this fact lies an important difference between a change in tastes and a change in expectations. A change in taste of course may also be due to experience, but it need not be. I may give up smoking a certain brand of cigarettes because I have found that it affects my throat, but I may also give it up because I no longer like it and 'have lost the taste for it'. There lies behind tastes an irreducible substrate which rational analysis cannot grasp, which may be of interest to the psychologist, but which defies the analytical tools of the economist.

Expectations, on the other hand, always embody *problematical* experience, i.e. an experience which requires *interpretation*. It is the task of the theory of expectations to elucidate the problems

20

our experience (and that of others in so far as it is accessible to us) sets us in judging the uncertain future, as well as to clarify the *modus interpretandi*. It is a task with which economists thus far do not seem to have come to grapple.

Experience is the raw material out of which all expectations are formed. But not all material is equally useful, not all experience is equally relevant to a given situation. There is a subjective element in the acts of the mind by which we select those portions of our experience we allow to affect our judgment of the future. But this *subjectivism of interpretation* is something altogether different from the *subjectivism of want* which underlies our utility theory. The former yields provisional judgments to be confirmed by later experience, imperfect knowledge capable of being perfected. The latter can provide us with no new knowledge: we either have a want or do not have it.

In a society based on division of labour men cannot act without knowing each other's needs and resources. Such knowledge need not be, as some have thought, 'perfect', but it must be relevant knowledge, knowledge of the demand and supply conditions in the markets in which one happens to deal. There is no difficulty in conceiving of such knowledge in a 'stationary state', a world without change, since here we need not ask how people came by their knowledge any more than we need ask how this improbable state of affairs came about: both belong to the category of, now irrelevant, 'bygones'.

But we can also conceive of a *quasi-stationary state* in which changes are few and far between, and each change has had its full repercussions before the next change takes place. This quasi-stationary state is the background of most neo-classical economics. Against it the method of comparative statics shows itself to full advantage. In this state knowledge is guided by prices functioning as signposts to action. Here it is by observing price changes that consumers learn which goods to substitute for which, and producers learn which line of production to abandon and which to turn to. Here we may say that the price system integrates all economic activity. We may regard the price system as a vast network of communications through which knowledge is at once transmitted from each market to the remotest corners of the economy. Every

c

significant change in needs or resources expresses itself in a price change, and every price change is a signal to consumers and producers to modify their conduct. Thus people gain knowledge about each other by closely following market prices.

But in the world in which we are living change does not follow such a convenient pattern. Here knowledge derived from price messages becomes problematical. It does not cease to be knowledge, but 'does not tell the whole story'. Many changes may happen simultaneously. Parts of our communications network may be 'jammed' and messages delayed. When a number of messages is received it is no longer clear in which order they were 'sent'. Moreover, even if there is no delay in transmission, today's knowledge may be out of date tomorrow, hence no longer a safe guide to action. Worst of all, in a world of continuous change much may be gained by those 'speculators' who prefer to anticipate tomorrow's changes today rather than adjust themselves to those recorded in the latest message received. Their action will affect prices which others take as their point of orientation, and which, if these speculators turn out to be wrong, may mislead others into actions they would not have taken had they known the real cause of the price change.

It is here neither necessary nor possible to follow up all the ramifications of the problem what constitutes relevant knowledge in a world of continuous change. This theme will be taken up again in Chapter IV. Action based on price messages conveying misleading information is, as we shall see in Chapter VII, often an important factor in the Trade Cycle.

For our present purpose it is sufficient to realize:

First, that in a world of continuous change prices are no longer in all circumstances a safe guide to action;

Second, that nevertheless even here price changes do transmit information, though now incomplete information;

Third, that such information therefore requires interpretation (the messages have to be 'decoded') in order to be transformed into knowledge, and all such knowledge is bound to be imperfect knowledge.

In a market economy success depends largely on the degree of refinement of one's instruments of interpretation. On the other hand, every act is a source of knowledge to others.

The formation of expectations is nothing but a phase in this continuous process of exchange and transmission of knowledge which effectively integrates a market society. A theory of expectations which can explain anything at all has therefore to start by studying this phase within the context of the process as a whole. If it fails to do this, it can accomplish nothing. Its first task is to describe the structure of the mental acts which constitute the formation of expectations; its second task, to describe the process of interaction of a number of individuals whose conduct is orientated towards each other.

For anybody who has to make a decision in the face of an uncertain future the formation of an expectation is *incidental* to the endeavour to diagnose the situation in which he has to act, an endeavour always undertaken with imperfect knowledge. The business man who forms an expectation is doing precisely what a scientist does when he formulates a working hypothesis. Both, business expectation and scientific hypothesis serve the same purpose; both reflect an attempt at cognition and orientation in an imperfectly known world, both embody imperfect knowledge to be tested and improved by later experience. Each expectation does not stand by itself but is the cumulative result of a series of former expectations which have been revised in the light of later experience, and these past revisions are the source of whatever present knowledge we have. On the other hand, our present expectation, to be revised later on as experience accrues, is not only the basis of the action plan but also a source of more perfect future knowledge. The formation of expectations is thus a continuous process, an element of the larger process of the transmission of knowledge. The rationale of the method of *process analysis*, as we shall learn in Chapter III, is that it enables us to treat the *ex ante* 'data' of action as provisional hypotheses to be revised in the light of later experience.

We have said that the formation of expectations is incidental to the diagnosis of the situation as a whole in which one has to act. How is this done? We analyse the situation, as we see it, in terms of *forces* to which we attribute various degrees of strength. We disregard what we believe to be *minor forces* and state our expectations in terms of the results we expect the operation of the *major forces* to have. Which forces we regard as major and minor is of course a matter of judgment. Here the subjective element of interpretation is seen at work. In general, we shall be inclined to treat forces working at random as minor forces, since we know nothing about their origin and direction, and are therefore anyhow unable to predict the result of their operation. We treat as major forces those about whose origin and direction we think we know something. This means that in assessing the significance of price changes observed in the past for future changes we shall tend to neglect those we believe to have been due to random causes, and to confine our attention to those we believe due to more 'permanent' causes. Hence, in a market economy, there are some price changes which transmit knowledge and are acted upon, and there are always others which are disregarded, often wrongly, and therefore become economically 'functionless'. This is an important distinction to which we shall return at the end of the chapter.

Having stated our expectations at the start of a 'period', we test them at its end by comparing actual with expected results, attempting to infer therefrom whether our initial diagnosis of forces and their strength was correct. This process, like all verification of hypotheses, is indirect and therefore often inconclusive. Again, it requires interpretation and yields imperfect knowledge. We may have been right for the wrong reason. Or, though we now may know that our original hypothesis was wrong, we do not know how we could have been right. The same result, say, a price change, may have been brought about by a number of different constellations of major forces, hence the need for further hypotheses and further testing.

Expectations are thus phases of a never-ending process, the process by which men acquire knowledge about each other's needs and resources. For our present purpose we shall draw three conclusions from this fact:

First, when at any point of time we look backwards at our past course of action we find that all our past expectations form a continuous sequence, whether they turned out to be right or wrong. For we learnt from all of them.

Second, there are problems of *consistency*, both interpersonal and intertemporal. Different people may hold different expectations at the same time; the same person may hold different expectations at different times. These are quite insoluble problems as long as we regard expectations as independent of each other. Why should they be consistent with each other?

But if we look at the process as a whole, the prospect becomes more hopeful; successful expectations, which stand the test, are, on the whole, more likely to reflect 'real forces' than unsuccessful expectations. And those whose expectations are never successful are likely to be eliminated by the market process. Moreover, as we shall see in Chapter IV, the market also tends to evolve institutions which mitigate interpersonal and intertemporal inconsistency.

Third, the results of past mistakes are there not merely to provide lessons, but to provide resources. In revising our expectations we not only have the knowledge, often dearly bought, of past mistakes (our own and others') to learn from, but also their physical counterpart, *malinvested capital*. Malinvested capital is still capital that can be adapted to other uses. This is the main problem of the theory of capital in a world of unexpected change. We shall come to deal with it in Chapter III.

Thus far we have endeavoured, all too briefly, to indicate at least some of the foundations on which, in our view, a theory of expectations which truly reflects economic processes which integrate a society founded on specialization and exchange, must be based. In the light of what we have thus learnt we shall now turn to a critical examination of some other attempts to present the problem of expectations in a systematic manner.

Until recently most studies of the problems of expectations were informed by the view that this is a proper field for the application of probability theory. An entrepreneur who has to make a decision the outcome of which is uncertain, is conceived of as setting up a probability distribution of possible quantitative outcomes for each course of action open to him. The next step is usually to 'substitute for the most probable prices actually expected with uncertainty equivalent prices expected with certainty'.[1] In this way the range of the probability distribution is compressed to a point, a 'certainty-equivalent'.[2] In 1945 we objected to this procedure on the

[1] Oscar Lange: *Price Flexibility and Employment*, p. 31.
[2] G. L. Shackle: *Expectations, Investment and Income*, 1938, p. 64.

ground that 'by subttituting single-value expectations for the uncertainty range of expected prices we stand to lose more than we gain, because reaction to price change will largely depend on the location of the prices affected within the scale of expected prices'.[3] We shall explain later on why we maintain this view.

But meanwhile the whole probability approach to the study of expectations has come under heavy fire. In the final chapter of his book *Expectations in Economics* [4] Professor Shackle has subjected what he calls the 'orthodox view' of the formation of expectations to strong and extensive criticism. His arguments are not new,[5] but they are none the less effective. His main point is 'the irrelevance of estimates of probability (in the sense of relative frequency) to unique or quasi-unique decisions'.[6] 'Few individual enterprises, for example, even in the course of their whole lives, launch a number of ventures of even broadly similar kinds which is "large" in any sense required by the theory, or even the practical application, of probability principles.' [7] The point is reinforced by the absence of a 'homogeneous universe of outcomes'. 'For many important kinds of decisions which must be taken in human affairs it will be impossible to find a sufficient number of past instances which occur under appropriately similar conditions; no well-founded figures of probability for different kinds of outcome can be established on the basis of experience.' [8]

Professor Shackle's criticism of the probability approach to the problem of expectations is sound enough, though the emphasis, in our view, should be on heterogeneity of situations rather than on uniqueness of decisions. It seems to us that Professor Shackle's argument might lose much of its applicability to the real world if the 'uniqueness of decisions' is taken too literally. Few business decisions are unique in the sense that they are made only once in a lifetime, and Professor Shackle only weakens his case by confining it to investment

[3] L. M. Lachmann: 'A Note on the Elasticity of Expectations', *Economica*, November 1945, p. 249.
[4] G. L. Shackle: *Expectations in Economics*, 1949.
[5] Cf. F. H. Knight: *Risk, Uncertainty and Profit*, Chapter VII, especially pp. 224–32, and L. v. Mises: *Human Action*, Chapter VI, especially pp. 106–15.
[6] G. L. Shackle: *Expectations in Economics*, 1949, p. 127.
[7] Ibid., p. 110.
[8] Ibid., pp. 109–10.

decisions involving very large sums.[9] We have to distinguish between uniqueness of decisions and uniqueness of the situations the decisions are taken to meet and to create. The number of possible business decisions is almost certainly smaller than the number of such possible situations, precisely because in an uncertain world each decision may have one of several results. And the 'outcomes' are here not, as in nature, 'external events given to us', but the result of a complex process of interaction always accompanied by transmission of knowledge. It therefore seems better to base our rejection of the probability theory of expectations on the inherent heterogeneity of the situations rather than on the uniqueness of decisions.

Whether Professor Shackle's positive contribution can be of much help to us in grappling with the problems set out earlier in this chapter must remain doubtful. The object of his study is the mental processes of an individual who has to take a decision in the face of an uncertain future. His theory is modelled on the equilibrium of the isolated individual (Robinson Crusoe) and stops there. It tells us nothing about market processes and nothing about the exchange and transmission of knowledge. To be sure 'a plan if it is to make sense must be based on one self-consistent scheme of expectations',[10] but the creation of such a scheme marks only the beginning of our problems. We have to ask how these expectations are formed, revised if disappointed, and projected into the future when successful. The changes of knowledge which Professor Shackle studies in his Chapter III imply a 'clarifying of expectations' in a purely formal sense. The events leading to such clarification are 'external events', not market transactions. In other words, Professor Shackle's is a static theory, and change is here comprehended as once-for-all change within the framework of comparative statics.

It is noteworthy that the only time that Professor Shackle mentions an actual market, this is a market which, for the time being, has ceased to function; a market not *in operation* but in *suspense*. In trying to account for a certain price phenomenon

---

[9] 'No business executive has to decide a hundred times in ten years whether or not to spend £1,000,000 on a new factory'—p. 115.
[10] Ibid., p. 111.

on the peri-urban land market he finds that 'Evidence taken
by the Uthwatt Committee shows that, where the belt of land
encircling a town is parcelled up amongst a large number of
separate ownerships, the market value of each piece is such
that when the separate values are aggregated, the total is
several times as great as would be warranted by any reasonable
estimate of *aggregate* future building development round the
town as a whole.   It is as though each actual and potential
owner of a plot of land near the town were convinced that,
out of a far more than adequate total supply of similarly situ-
ated land, the particular plot in question was almost *certain*
to be selected as part of the site for such new houses as will be
required during, say, the next twenty years.' [11]

Professor Shackle regards this as a 'curious phenomenon'
and attempts an explanation in terms of his 'potential surprise
functions'.   But a much simpler explanation can be given in
terms of the market process, or rather, its conspicuous absence
in this case.

The function of the capital market is to allocate scarce capital
resources amongst a number of alternative uses.   This is simple
where these uses are known, not so simple where they are not
known.   For them to be known, however, it is not enough
merely that the total quantity required is known.   Where
these uses are specific, unless individual uses and their specific
requirements are known, no allocation can take place.

In the case under discussion this is just what has happened:
while total requirements can be estimated, individual future
requirements are unknown.   On the other hand, the need of
land for urban development is the most important need.   In
this situation the market safeguards the future provision for
the most important need by *suspending* the allocation to others
and creating a reserve stock of land.   This it does by making
the price of each plot equal to its value in satisfying the most
important need, thus making it impossible for anybody who
wants land for other purposes, to get it.   The need for a reserve
stock will continue until the individual and specific needs are
known.   Then, but only then, the market process of allocation
can begin.   '*Market*', *in the true economic sense, means a process of
exchange and allocation reflecting the transmission of knowledge*.   It

[11] G. L. Shackle: *Expectations in Economics*, 1949, p. 91.   (His italics.)

does not simply mean that prices are quoted. The prices quoted may be what they are in order to prevent, and not to facilitate, dealings. Where this is the case we have a *market in suspense*, not a *market in operation*. Professor Shackle, like the experts of the Uthwatt Committee, has become the victim of verbal confusion.

From this example it may be seen that the theory of expectations neglects the market process at its peril.

After this critical digression we must turn to a more constructive task. The reader, before whom we set certain ideas about expectations in the early part of this chapter, will no doubt expect us to give concrete shape to these ideas by embodying them in an analytical framework within which concrete problems can be solved and actual market processes rendered intelligible.[12] But there is another reason, intrinsic to our argument, why we should make an attempt in this direction.

We have described a market economy in motion as an imperfect communications network. There are, however, important economic changes which do not find their expression in price changes. They constitute the phenomenon of *price inflexibility* about which we shall have to say something in Chapter IV. There are also price changes which do not reflect major economic changes. We said above that in a market economy there are some price changes which transmit knowledge and are acted upon, and there are always others which are disregarded, often wrongly, and therefore become economically 'functionless'.[13] Evidently it is of great importance to us to find a generalization on which an adequate criterion of distinction between 'significant' (meaningful) and 'functionless' (meaningless) price movements can be based. If such a generalization could not be found it would become impossible to hold that prices integrate the market economy. All we could say would be: some do and some do not. There are many difficulties of course in finding such a generalization, foremost among which is one which directly reflects what we

[12] It is true that for the main purpose of this book, the elucidation of a morphological conception of capital, this may not seem strictly necessary. But, as will be seen in Chapter IV, it may be of help in making us understand the distinction between *consistent* and *inconsistent* capital change.

[13] See above, p. 24.

have called the subjectivism of interpretation: the same price movement may be meaningful to one, and meaningless to another person. Nevertheless it seems to us possible to construct an analytical framework within which:

   a. the distinction between meaningful and meaningless price movements can be given a clear meaning, and
   b. the distinction can be seen to be practically significant: meaningful and meaningless price movements do in fact have different results.

It may even be possible to link the distinction with that between minor ('random') and major ('permanent') forces. We might say, for instance, that the market will tend to disregard price changes believed to be due to random causes while paying close attention to those it believes prompted by a change in the constellation of fundamental forces.

Such an analytical framework we find in what, following Dr. Lange, we call 'The Practical Range'.[14]

Let us suppose that on a market a 'set of self-consistent expectations' has had time to crystallize and to create a conception of a 'normal price range'. Suppose that any price between £95 and £110 would be regarded as more or less 'normal', while a wider range of prices, say from £80 to £125, would be regarded as *possible*. We thus have two ranges, an 'inner range' from 95 to 110 reflecting the prevailing conception of 'normality', and an 'outer range' associated with what is regarded as possible price change. Many economists have started their study of expectations with the notion of a 'range', usually in the form of a probability distribution, but only to discard it at the next moment in favour of a point, a 'certainty-equivalent', 'to substitute for the most probable prices actually expected with uncertainty equivalent prices expected with certainty'.[15] By contrast, we shall endeavour to show that the location and motion of actual prices within our ranges are of crucial importance for the formation of expectations, and that by compressing the range to a point we should lose the very frame of reference within which actual price changes can alone be meaningfully interpreted and shown to be relevant to the formation of expectations.

[14] Lange, op. cit., p. 30.   [15] Ibid., p. 31.

What is the significance of our two ranges for the formation and revision of expectations?

As long as actual prices move well within the inner range, between, say, 96 and 109, such price movements will probably be regarded as insignificant and due to random causes. In fact, where the 'normality' conception is strongly entrenched, it will be very difficult for the price to pass the limits. For as soon as the price approaches the upper or lower limit of the inner range, people will think that the movement 'cannot go much farther' and, anticipating a movement in reverse, will sell (near the upper limit) or buy (near the lower limit). In such a situation 'inelastic expectations' will tend to 'stabilize' prices within the inner range.

But suppose that in spite of sales pressure near the upper, and buying pressure near the lower limit, price either rises above 110 or falls below 95. Such an event will sooner or later give rise to second thoughts. As long as actual prices move within the outer range, between 110 and 125, or 80 and 95, it is true, nothing has happened which was not regarded as possible. But the more thoughtful market operators will take heed. The mere fact that in spite of the heavy 'speculative' pressure encountered near the limits of the inner range, and engendered by inelastic expectations and the sense of the 'normality' of the inner range, price could pass these limits at all is a pointer to the strength of the forces which must have carried it past such formidable obstacles. Such a movement can hardly be due to random causes.

But the force that carried the price past the limits, while strong, need not be a permanent force. It may spend itself sooner or later. The market will therefore judge the significance of price movements within the outer range by the supplementary criterion of the time factor. If prices relapse soon and return to the inner range this will of course confirm the prevailing notion of normality. But if they stay within the outer range, gradually opinion will swing round. First some, and then others, will come to revise their notion of 'normal price'. Such revision will express itself in a new willingness to buy at a price, say 118, at which formerly one would have sold, or to sell at a price, say 88, at which formerly one would have bought. This means that a price movement, once it has been strong enough to overcome resistant pressure at the limits of the inner range, and reached the outer range, will probably sooner or later be carried further by the very speculative forces which formerly resisted it. This is readily seen if we reflect that the sales and purchases near the limits must have been at the expense of normal stocks, so that a price of 115 would probably now find the market with low stocks, and a price of 90 with an accumulation of excess stocks which are now a mere relic of the unsuccessful speculation of the 'normalists'. A fast movement within the outer range may therefore be just as much due to re-stocking (positive or negative) as to the operation of more permanent forces. This is why in such a situation the market keeps a close eye on stock variations.[16] In fact, in dynamic conditions price movements have always to be interpreted with an eye on the 'statistical position' of the market which thus becomes a second supplementary criterion for diagnosis.

Once the price passes the limits of the outer range, rises above 125 or falls below 80, an entirely new situation faces us. The market, shocked out of its sense of normality, will have to revise its diagnosis of the permanent forces governing a 'normal situation'. It must now become clear to everybody that the hypothesis about the constellation of fundamental forces which formed the basis of our range structure has been tested and has failed. But while the failure of an experiment may invalidate a hypothesis, it does not by itself suggest a new one. It follows by no means that the really operative forces will be recognized at once. That must depend on the insight, vigilance, and intelligence of the market. Experience shows, for instance, that an inflation is hardly ever recognized as such in its initial stages, at least in a society which has no prior experience of it. Almost invariably, at one point or another in this early phase, people will think that prices are already 'too high', will defer purchases and postpone investment plans. In this way, they will, by their very failure to understand the *modus operandi* of the fundamental force, mitigate its impact for a time by reducing 'effective demand'. And if, as is not impossible, the inflation stops early enough, they

[16] Cf. L. M. Lachmann: 'Commodity Stocks and Equilibrium', *Review of Economic Studies*, June 1936.

may be right after all!   But it is more likely that they will be wrong.   And in so far as their action entails the undermaintenance of capital, the ultimate results for society may well be disastrous.

We may conclude that price movements within the inner range will be disregarded and thus be 'functionless'.   Price change beyond the limits of the inner range may or may not be meaningful, but judgment will here have to depend on supplementary criteria such as the time factor and concomitant variations in the size of stocks.   It is only when prices move beyond the outer range altogether that they become unquestionably 'meaningful', can no longer be disregarded, and convey a 'message'.   But while the negative content of the message is clear enough, viz. the invalidation of the hypothesis which formed the basis of the former range structure, its positive content is less so.   The message still requires interpretation, and this will depend upon the insight and intelligence of the men in the market.

Our concept of the Range Structure, composed of inner and outer range, seems thus vindicated as a useful tool of analysis, and our refusal to exchange it for a 'certainty-equivalent' would appear to be justified.   For our concept permits us to draw a distinction between price phenomena which are consistent with the existing structure of expectations, fall 'within the ranges', and thus cause no disappointment, and, on the other hand, phenomena inconsistent with the existing structure of expectations, which fall 'outside the ranges' a revision of which they necessitate.   We noticed that as long as the price movement is confined to within the inner range it does not provide relevant new information but merely confirms the soundness of the diagnosis which found its expression in the existence of this range, while movements within the outer range provide information of problematical value which, to be useful, has to be supplemented by observation of other phenomena.   As soon, however, as the price moves beyond the limits of the outer range, the inadequacy of the diagnosis on which the ranges were based becomes patent.   A new situation has arisen which requires a new diagnosis and thus a new mental effort.

It remains true that, by and large, price changes integrate a market economy by spreading new knowledge.   But not all price changes are equally significant in this respect. Their significance has to be assessed with respect to a 'given' structure of expectations which finds its expression in a system of ranges. Their practical effect will depend on how quickly the men in the market come to understand what has happened and revise their expectations. To impede price change is therefore to withhold knowledge from the market. On the other hand, it is possible to have 'misleading' price movements. About them more will be said in later chapters.

CHAPTER III

PROCESS ANALYSIS AND CAPITAL THEORY

The theory of capital has to start from the fact that the capital goods with which entrepreneurs operate are heterogeneous. These heterogeneous capital goods have to be used together. Heterogeneity here implies complementarity in use. The mode of this complementarity, the proportions in which the various heterogeneous factors of production are being used for a given purpose, must find its expression in the Production Plan. Each such plan is characterized by the coefficients of production of its input and the output result it envisages. But while the output result is at first merely planned, the decision about coefficients of production has to be made at once; otherwise there can be no plan.

If the plan fails it has to be revised. The coefficients of production will thus be affected.[1] Some labour will be dismissed, other labour may be taken on. The same happens to capital goods. Some are discarded, others acquired. A revision of a plan will as a rule involve *capital regrouping*, a variation in the mode of complementarity of the capital goods used.

The theory of capital has to explain why capital goods are being used in the way they are. Their mode of use depends on the complementarity pattern of resource use reflected in the various production plans, a pattern which varies with the successes and failures of these plans. The theory of capital must therefore concern itself with the way in which entrepreneurs form combinations of heterogeneous capital resources in their plans, *and* the way in which they regroup them when they revise these plans. A theory which ignores such regrouping ignores a highly significant aspect of reality: the changing pattern of resource use which the divergence of results actually experienced from what they had been expected to be, imposes on entrepreneurs.

---

[1] The criterion of success or failure, as we pointed out in the last chapter, has to be sought within the expectational framework of the plan.

That to the planning entrepreneur his capital resources are primarily given in their heterogeneity, as buildings, machines, tools, etc., may seem obvious to the reader. Unfortunately this fact is at variance with the main trend of the traditional theory of capital which treats capital as a homogeneous value magnitude expressed in money terms. No doubt this notion of capital corresponds in many ways to the concept of capital actually used in business life, in particular in its accounting and financial aspects. It may therefore seem worthwhile to point out that for our purposes in this chapter, the description of the formation and revision of capital combinations in production plans, these business uses of the word 'capital' are irrelevant.

It is true of course that every enterprise has to start with a sum of homogeneous money capital, 'free capital'. But the collection of the money capital from owners and creditors belongs to a phase which logically (if not actually: the technical blueprints may already be in existence) precedes the making of the production plan. As we shall learn in Chapter VI, it is true that what happens during the 'financing stage' of an enterprise is not entirely irrelevant to what happens later on: the 'control structure' may well influence later decisions, for instance about expansion or reconstruction. But as long as we are concerned with the making of the production plan and the building-up of the capital combination on which it rests, all this is irrelevant. After all, one cannot earn a profit on capital without 'investing' it, and that means to de-homogenize money capital.

It is also true that all the time there will exist a capital account in which the various capital resources appear as a homogeneous value aggregate. But the capital account within the precincts of which we reduce our capital resources to a common denominator, is merely an institutional device for testing success or failure. We use it to test the result of the plan, not to operate the plan. Changes in the total value of assets, to be sure, are our measure of success, but they cannot tell us what happened or why, any more than a thermometer can tell us whether the patient suffers from malaria or influenza.

The path of economic progress is strewn with the wreckage of failures. Every business man knows this, but few economists

seem to have taken note of it.   In most of the theories currently
in fashion economic progress is apparently regarded as the
more or less automatic outcome of capital investment, 'autonomous' or otherwise.   Perhaps we should not be surprised at
this fact: mechanistic theories are bound to produce results
which look automatic.

The view which, by establishing a functional relationship
between them, practically identifies progress with capital
accumulation, rests on at least three fallacies.   In the first
place, capital accumulation is not the only force engendering progress; the division of labour and changes in technical
knowledge are others.   Sometimes these three forces support
each other, but often they offset each other as, for instance,
when changing technical knowlege makes specific skills or
specific equipment redundant.   Secondly, as we shall learn
in Chapter V, even where capital accumulation appears to
engender an increase in output, this is in many cases not the
direct result of merely quantitative change, but its indirect
result, and the direct result of a concomitant change in the
composition of capital.

But the most egregious fallacy of the view which identifies
capital accumulation with progress is surely its complete disregard of the facts of malinvestment.   The fact that in modern
industrial countries progress is accompanied by annual net
investment must not make us forget that a good deal of the
new capital value will be lost before its planned depreciation
period is over.   A realistic theory of capital has to ask why
this is so, and what processes in the sphere of production and
planning the change in capital value reflects.

The loss in value of course reflects the fact that capital
instruments, particularly those that are durable, have to be
used in ways other than those for which they were designed.
In these new uses the instruments may be either more or less
profitable than in their designed uses.   In the former case
there will be a gain, in the latter a loss of value, i.e. their
market value will differ from their cost of production.   The
cause of the phenomenon is unexpected change.   Hence,
durable capital goods are more likely to be affected than those
more short-lived.   In the case of buildings our phenomenon
often occurs for the simple reason that they last for longer

D

periods than could possibly enter any plan-maker's 'horizon'. Often, as we stroll in the streets of an ancient town, the merchants' palaces turned into hotels, the former stables now garages, and the old warehouses which have become modern workshops, remind us of the impossibility of planning for the remote future. In this case our phenomenon, viz. the fact that capital goods are not used in accordance with the plans originally made for them, is the mere result of the passage of time. Here only the most durable goods will be affected.

In modern industrial economies, however, rapid technical progress and the growing predominance of durable capital equipment have brought a very large proportion of capital resources within the scope of our phenomenon. In such a world there can be few fixed capital goods which year after year are used in the same manner. Dr. Terborgh has illustrated this fact by

the life history of a freight locomotive of the vintage, say, of 1890. It began in heavy main-line service. After a few years, the improvement in the new locomotives available and the development of the art of rail-roading made the unit obsolete for that service, which was taken over by more modern power. It was thereupon relegated to branch-line duty where the trains were shorter, the speeds lower, and the annual mileage greatly reduced. For some years it served in that capacity, but better power was continually being displaced from main-line duty and 'kicked downstairs' onto the branch lines, and eventually our locomotive was forced out at the bottom, to become a switcher in one of the tanktown yards along the line. But the march of progress was relentless, and, in the end, thanks to the combination of obsolescence and physical deterioration, it wound up on the inactive list. For some years more it lay around, idle most of the time, but pressed into service during seasonal traffic peaks and special emergencies. Finally, at long last, the bell tolled and it passed off the scene to the scrap heap.[2]

If, then, at each moment we must expect to find capital goods used in ways other than those for which they were originally planned, a realistic theory of capital cannot altogether ignore these facts. We must make an attempt to trace the

[2] By permission from *Dynamic Equipment Policy*, by George Terborgh. Copyright 1949. McGraw-Hill Book Company, Inc., p. 17.

process by which these changes in capital take place, and by 'tracing' we mean showing how cause becomes effect and effect new cause. It is readily seen that for this purpose the method of equilibrium analysis is of but little use. Equilibrium analysis can tell us whether courses of action are, or are not, consistent with each other. It cannot, except in rather special circumstances, explain how inconsistencies are removed. These special circumstances would require that all possible forms of action can be described in the form of continuous functions which do not vary as the inconsistencies are discovered and spell failure. They require, in other words, downward-sloping demand curves, upward-sloping supply curves and a point of intersection between them. As we shall see, there is no reason to believe that such continuous functions can exist in the market for capital goods. To trace the process of changing capital use we shall have to apply the method of Process Analysis to the use of capital resources.

Most economists are now familiar with the method of Process Analysis as expounded in the writings of Hicks,[3] Lindahl[4] and Lundberg.[5] It is a causal-genetic method of studying economic change, tracing the effects of decisions made independently of each other by a number of individuals through time, and showing how the incompatibility of these decisions after a time necessitates their revision. In order to appreciate its merits we have to contrast it with the method of study it is designed to supersede, or at least to supplement, i.e. equilibrium analysis.

In equilibrium analysis our interest is confined to plans which are consistent with each other. We assume that consumers, producers, investors, etc., have a large number of alternative plans, so large a number indeed that these plans can be analytically described in terms of continuous functions, or graphically depicted as curves or surfaces. From these plans we select those which are consistent with each other, disregarding all others. In fact, the whole system of human action is here described not in terms of the network of operative plans of which it is in reality the final outcome, but in terms of a

[3] J. R. Hicks: *Value and Capital*, 1939.
[4] Erik Lindahl: *Studies in the Theory of Money and Capital*, 1939, in particular Part One, pp. 21–138.
[5] Erik Lundberg: *Studies in the Theory of Economic Expansion*, Stockholm and London, 1937, especially Chapter IX.

small cross-section of plans which happens to lend itself to mathematical treatment. Justification for this procedure is sought in the fact that inconsistent plans of individuals who stand in exchange relationships with each other cannot succeed, and that the resultant failures will necessitate continual revision of plans, until a consistent set of plans has been discovered. In this view, then, economic activity consists largely in the testing of plans for mutual consistency. While this takes time, we have to assume that during the 'period of adjustment' nothing happens that may disturb our original data expressed as alternative plans. While the failure of each successive plan conveys significant additional knowledge to the individuals concerned, it does not affect the shape of the demand and supply curves. It merely induces individual actors to choose other points on them for testing. It is usually assumed that as a result of the accumulating experience gained from a series of unsuccessful tests, a consistent solution is sure to be found in the end, in other words, that in the 'real world' there does exist a 'tendency towards equilibrium'.

In process analysis, on the other hand, we need no such assumption. While retaining the postulate of consistent action for each actor, we no longer assume that the acts of large numbers of people will be consistent with each other. On the contrary, we take interpersonal inconsistency for granted and study its effects. Process analysis, we may say, combines the equilibrium of the decision-making unit, firm or household, with the disequilibrium of the market. There is a good reason for this assumption: The human mind is an instrument for reducing chaos to order. All those acts which are inspired by the same mind are therefore unlikely to display chaotic inconsistency. Whatever number of acts a mind can control it can also bring into consistency, and as consistency of action is a necessary, though not of course sufficient, condition of success in action, the mind will have to do so. But beyond this sphere of manifestations of the individual mind, outside the firm and household, no such agent exists. It is true of course that the market serves to produce interpersonal consistency, but it does so *indirectly* by modifying the conditions of action of the individuals. The market is no substitute for the decision-making unit. Precisely in order to explain how market phenomena affect decisions we require that interpretation of experience, constituted by acts of the mind, which we discussed in Chapter II.

It will be remembered that the classical economists, who of course were only concerned with firms and not with households, had an additional institutional safeguard to ensure interpersonal consistency: the bankruptcy court. All those unable to equate average cost and price are supposed to disappear sooner or later from the scene of economic action. Only those able to adjust themselves to existing conditions would continue to act. But the extension of the theory of the firm to cases other than those of competition, and in general the extension of economic analysis to the household, and that is to say, to everybody, have deprived this case of its former significance.

The method of process analysis which lends itself to the treatment of micro- as well as macro-economic problems, has thus far been mainly applied to the explanation of pricing, production, and saving-investment-spending decisions. In what follows we shall use it in order to elucidate the dynamic implications of decisions about the use of capital resources.

Every resource has a number of possible uses. The best use will, in each instance, depend on a number of circumstances, for instance, the relative prices of input and output. The owner of a capital resource will thus, in arriving at a decision about its use, have to compare the prices, present and expected, of the various kinds of output it could produce, with the wages, present and expected, of the various types of labour that could produce it. But a capital resource in isolation can produce no output. Every decision about its use will therefore imply decisions about the use of other resources *complementary* to it.

Often of course it will be possible to produce different kinds of output from the same capital combination (plant, machinery, working capital, etc.) for instance, by varying labour input. Then that output will be produced which maximizes profits, and any experience calculated to induce the belief that the current production plan does not do this will lead to a revision of the plan. But the range of outputs which might possibly be produced will always increase if possible variations of the existing capital combination are taken into account. In a market economy a firm can always vary its capital combination by buying and selling capital goods. Hence, each firm will intermittently use the market in order to acquire those capital instruments which, when operated by the labour available at current wage rates, will maximize profits. The firm will pay for its purchases by discarding those capital goods which in the new combination are no longer required.

In what follows we shall assume that each firm has one plant which during the period under investigation it neither sells nor enlarges.[6] In combination with its plant it uses capital equipment of various types. The proportions in which the various types of equipment are combined with the plant, what we shall call 'the capital coefficients', are embodied in the production plan. A plan cannot be changed during a period, while it can and probably will be revised at the end of it. The capital coefficients are thus rigidly fixed for each plan, but flexible for longer periods. Even so, however, we shall assume that the number of possible capital combinations from which the firm has to choose is limited. While the mode of complementarity may change from period to period, the relationship between most capital resources is usually one of complementarity.

There is, however, one important exception from this rule. Every plan has to make provision for unforeseen contingencies. Certain factors have to be kept in reserve (spare parts, excess stocks, etc.) to be thrown into action if and when necessary. The extent to which they will be used is not known in advance; hence, these quantities are not amongst the fixed coefficients of production in the plan. Indeed their variability is the very reason for their existence. To what extent they will become complementary to the factors of production actually in operation depends on chance. It might therefore be better to speak of *supplementary* capital goods to distinguish them from the components of the capital combinations.

These supplementary resources have an interesting property: the record of their quantitative change can be used as a primary test of success or failure. Depletion of the reserves is a sure mark of failure. Even in less extreme cases the need of using reserves will increase costs and reduce net profit.

Among the firm's resources the use of which is plotted in

[6] This assumption will be abandoned in Chapter VI.

the plan, money capital has a peculiar part to play. That money capital which will be used during the plan period to pay wages, purchase raw materials, etc., must not be regarded as capital for our purpose, as otherwise we should be guilty of double-counting. If we think of the coal used for production during our plan period as a capital good, of its quantity as a capital coefficient, we cannot at the same time call the money paid for it 'capital'. If labour is a factor of production and a component element of the plan, the money laid out to pay for it cannot simultaneously be capital. At most we might say that at the start of the plan money capital 'stands proxy' for those factors of production who are part of the plan but scheduled to appear on the stage later on.

But not all the money at the firm's disposal is allotted to such specific uses. Some of it is not planned to be used at all. It forms the *cash reserve* which has the same general function as all reserves: to be thrown into action in case of unforeseen contingencies. The cash reserve is therefore capital in the same way, and for the same reason, as spare parts are. While such money is 'idle', its idleness is a condition of successful action.

All these supplementary goods have to be more or less perfect substitutes for those goods actually in operation which, if need be, they are to replace. This fact has given rise to the need for the standardization of equipment, a device for keeping the size of such supplementary stocks within manageable proportions. In this respect money, the universal substitute, is superior to almost all others as, if necessary, it can be exchanged for any other good currently on the market.

Unplanned variations in the stock of money are highly significant primary tests of success or failure of business plans. The ultimate measure of business success is, of course, the balance sheet as a whole. But as profit will as a rule accrue in the money form, and since the cash reserve is mostly the central reserve which no serious failure can leave unaffected, success and failure are likely to be recorded by changes in the cash reserve before being recorded anywhere else.

While for the period of the plan most coefficients are fixed, each plan must allow for some flexibility. Variations of the variable factors thus convey currently information about how the plan is going. If *all* factors were rigidly fixed there would be no variable element left to record success or failure.

Let us suppose that during a period t_1 a firm has a capital combination of the form

$$kA + lB + mC \quad . \quad . \quad . \quad . \quad . \quad (1)$$

where A, B, C . . . are different types of equipment and k, l, m . . . are constants.

At the end of period t_1, in the light of experience gained during ·the period it is decided to alter the combination. Some of this experience may be 'purely technical knowledge' about the capacity of our combination to achieve, with the help of the labour force assigned to it, in the production plan for t_1, the 'output targets' set for it in the plan. In this case the economic significance of the technical knowledge thus gained is quite unambiguous and its meaning for future production plans obvious. But some of the experience of period t_1 is marketing experience, which cannot be used for future planning without interpretation of the kind discussed in Chapter II.

Let us now suppose that in the light of all the circumstances regarded as relevant to planning of the future, it is decided in period t_2 to change the combination (1) into another combination

$$l'B + m'C + nD \quad . \quad . \quad . \quad . \quad . \quad (2)$$

where l is smaller than l' and m larger than m', and D a type of equipment not hitherto used by the firm. The firm will therefore have to sell kA and $(m - m')C$ and buy $(l' - l)B$ and nD. Assuming no net investment or disinvestment we, may suppose that

$$kA + (m - m')C = nD + (l' - l)B \quad . \quad . \quad (3)$$

Let us now assume that at the end of t_1 each entrepreneur revises his production plan for t_2 and his capital combination. At once we have to ask what determines the prices of the capital goods thus discarded and acquired. At a first glance it might appear that the problem can be solved within the traditional framework of equilibrium analysis. For each entrepreneur, it seems, there will be minimum prices below which he. will not sell, for instance because he expects that if he waits until t_3 he will get a better price. And there will be maximum prices of capital goods above which he will not buy, as at prices above them (2) will not be an optimum combination. Somewhere between these maxima and minima it might seem that the interplay of the market would establish equilibrium prices for each category of capital equipment. Thus we might be led to believe that on a 'market day' which marks the beginning of t_2 a 'temporary equilibrium' of the market for capital goods will establish itself.

At closer inspection, however, it is seen that the position is not determinate and equilibrium analysis not applicable.

In the first place, the assumption that each firm will be able to finance the reshuffle of its capital combinations without having to draw on its cash reserve or outside sources seems far removed from reality. There appears to be no reason to believe that the proceeds of the sale of the instruments discarded will always just suffice to buy the new instruments. If so, (3) is not valid. We might assume that firms count with the fact that the sale of old equipment will not cover the purchase price of the new equipment, and plan to make up for the difference by drawing on their cash reserves. Then we have

$$kA + (m - m')C + z = nD + (l' - l)B \quad . \quad . \quad (4)$$

where z is the diminution of the cash reserve. In general, the new capital combination will be chosen in such a way that if a is the expected average profit from it,

$$\frac{a}{kA + (m - m')C + z}$$

is maximized.

If n firms reshuffle their capital combinations, then, as long as they sell their discarded equipment to each other, i.e. as long as no new equipment is bought nor any old equipment sold for scrap, we would have

$$z_1 + z_2 + z_3 + \ldots + zn = 0 \quad . \quad . \quad . \quad (5)$$

where z_1 is the cash reduction of firm 1, z_2 of firm 2, etc. In this case clearly some of the z's must be negative. Some firms will find themselves with an actual cash surplus after having completed the operation.

Now, the fundamental difficulty which makes it impossible to apply equilibrium analysis to our case, lies in the fact that the regrouping decisions of the various firms need not be consistent with each other.   If they are not, some of them cannot be carried out.   This dilemma expresses itself in the fact that, on the one hand, the regrouping decisions are based on the assumption of certain prices for new equipment bought and old equipment sold, while, on the other hand, these prices cannot be known before the process of exchange is completed. In other words, our firms do not know in advance what they will get or have to pay, yet they have to make their plans which involve acts of exchange in advance of the actual carrying-out of these plans.   Prices expected may not be realized, and realized prices not be such as would make a particular regrouping decision profitable.

It is not a way out of our dilemma to postulate that each firm starts with a number of alternative plans depending on buying and selling prices in the market.   In the first place, there is still no reason why among this large number of probably inconsistent plans there should be at least one set of plans (one for each regrouping firm) which would be consistent. Moreover, even if this were so, even if we could draw supply and demand curves and get 'points of intersection', there is the fact that we have not one market but a number of markets, in fact as many markets as there are types of goods to be exchanged.   These supply and demand curves, even if they were continuous, would not be independent of each other since the prices at which goods are offered or demanded are not independent of each other.   If the A-goods, for example, fetch higher prices, higher offers can be made for D-goods, and vice versa.   We know from general equilibrium theory that such circumstances are sufficient to make prices in each market indeterminate unless we either assume that all prices are fixed simultaneously or permit Edgeworthian re-contract.   For the sake of realism we can admit neither.   Hence, the results of earlier transactions will influence prices in later transactions. Prices thus come to depend on the chronological order of transactions, and this order is of course quite arbitrary.   On the other hand, there must be such an order. As there can be no sales without purchases, we cannot assume for instance that all firms sell their old machines first and then form the new combinations on the basis of prices realized.

There is one escape from our dilemma which would enable firms to carry out their regrouping decisions 'according to plan'. But if we choose it we cannot possibly call the position reached at the end of the operation an 'equilibrium position'. Let us assume that there are 'given' prices for new equipment and 'given' scrap prices for old, prices which would not be affected by dealings in the second-hand market. Let us further assume that each regrouping firm bases its policy on what Professor Neisser has termed 'The Strategy of Expecting the Worst': it expects neither to get more than the scrap price for the equipment it discards nor to be able to buy equipment in the second-hand market, but to have to buy new equipment at the current price. In this way the 'ceiling' price for new equipment and the 'floor' price for old form the basis of its plan. And if we assume that the scrap price would not be affected by our regrouping (a doubtful assumption) and that the (ex factory) prices of new equipment are sufficiently rigid not to be affected by demand arising from regrouping (a somewhat more realistic assumption in the world of modern industry), these plans might be feasible.

But the 'strategy of expecting the worst', while it may be the safest, is not necessarily the 'best' policy. The position reached as the result of carrying out these plans cannot be called an *optimum* position for the firm. To be sure, if all firms base their plans on the 'worst possibility', almost all of them will make 'gains'. To the extent to which the market offers them terms more favourable than were envisaged in their plans, their actual 'z', the draft on the cash reserves actually experienced, will be less than the planned 'z'. Indeed for some of them their actual 'z' may become negative if they find they can sell their old machines at prices much higher than the scrap price and buy machines on the second-hand market much below the 'new' price. But the fact remains that, had they known in advance on what terms they would be able to trade in the second-hand market, they would have made regrouping decisions other than they actually did.

Two conclusions, one negative and one positive, emerge from what has been said. First, equilibrium analysis must not be applied to capital regrouping. Regrouping decisions are unlikely to be consistent with each other, and even where they are, firms may yet find themselves, when the operation is completed, in a position they would not have chosen had they known what alternatives were open to them. The reshuffling of capital combinations, whatever its motives and consequences, is not a 'return to equilibrium'. The very acts it implies are likely to have new disequilibrating effects.

Secondly, and this is our positive conclusion, capital regrouping has to be treated as a dynamic phenomenon similar to the processes which give rise to it. In it, as in everything else, firms might succeed or fail. Their relative strength in their new ventures will be affected by the measure of success they have achieved in regrouping. A negative 'z', for instance, will mean greater financial strength. A piece of machinery may have been bought so cheaply that it can be used profitably for purposes other than those envisaged in the regrouping plan. If so, it may entail further purchases of complementary capital equipment. In any case, what happens in period t_2 is not the mere result of what happened in t_1, nor the result of what happened in t_1 plus the decisions made at its end. It will be the combined result of events during t_1, plan revisions at its end, and the success with which these decisions met before t_2 even began.

We now have to take account of some of the repercussions our process will have. The existence of maximum prices means of course that at them new capital goods will be brought into our capital combinations, and if minimum prices are set by scrap values, some of our old capital goods will be turned into scrap rather than change hands. But there will now also be goods kept in physical existence, though not in productive use, in the hope of higher prices in the future, just as equilibrium price does not preclude the existence of unsold goods that would be offered at higher prices. While the 'strategy of expecting the worst' requires a 'floor' price, this need not be the scrap price.

When looking at the new combinations we shall thus find among them some new capital goods the sale of which is not the result of past failure, but the result of the fact that prices of similar existing goods have reached the upper limit.   Conversely we shall find, but not as part of our new combinations, some disused equipment which is not turned into scrap since the owners expect its future value to exceed present scrap prices, perhaps because they expect scrap prices to rise, perhaps because they can foresee more favourable conditions for future use.   This is the 'idle capacity' which in the 1930's gave rise to so much misunderstanding and the importance of which for dynamic theory has now been discovered by Mrs. Robinson [7] and others.   It is usually regarded as the result of 'lack of effective demand'.   But this is only half an explanation. What we need to know is not merely why capital is not used in the way it was planned to be used, but why no alternative use has been found for it.

Looking at the matter in the way we have done also opens up a new vista on the problem of the 'incentive to invest'. New capital goods are being used in combination with existing ones.   This form of complementarity means that the lower the price of existing capital goods the greater the profitability of the new goods.   In the theory of investment currently in fashion, to be sure, complementarity is never mentioned. Economists, making an economic virtue of accounting necessity, have uncritically taken over the accounting convention which treats all capital as homogeneous.

In the real world, however, entrepreneurs have to combine buildings, plant, equipment, etc., and the success of the production plans embodying these combinations determines how long they will be maintained.   This whole set of problems must remain concealed from a theory which treats all capital as homogeneous.   Investment then becomes merely a question of changing the absolute quantity of this homogeneous capital stock.   Its *composition* does not interest the economist whose theory of investment is bound to be somewhat fragmentary.

Yet it is surely plain that, just as the profitability of all capital goods in a combination depends *inter alia* on the wages of the co-operant labour, so the rate of profit on each capital good depends on the cost at which complementary capital goods can be secured.   The 'marginal efficiency of investment',

[7] Joan Robinson: *The Rate of Interest and Other Essays*, 1952, especially pp. 77–80.

i.e. the expected profitability of new capital goods, depends *inter alia* on the prices at which existing capital goods can be obtained in the market. The lower the latter the higher the former.

Keynes, to be sure, did not neglect the effect of the prices of existing capital goods on new investment, but, treating in characteristic fashion all capital as homogeneous, only saw the possibility of substitution. So he held that prices of existing capital goods below reproduction cost would weaken the incentive to invest. But in reality capital is as a rule heterogeneous and complementary. Except in the case, which Keynes alone considered, where existing and new capital goods happen to be substitutes, low prices of the former will have a favourable effect on the incentive to invest. Neglect of the heterogeneity of capital thus vitiates the theory of investment.[8]

What has thus far been said in this chapter also throws some light on certain problems in the theory of money. This is not the place to discuss fully the role of money in the Theory of Assets. We have already learned something about the function of the cash reserve in the execution of the production plan; and more will be said about money as an asset in Chapter VI. But meanwhile we may consider the relevance of capital regrouping to the distinction between 'active' and 'idle' money which is so fundamental to the Keynesian theory of money.

Where firms have to draw on their cash reserves or borrow from outside sources in order to finance regrouping, it might seem at a first glance that 'idle' money is brought into circulation and 'activated'. Now, in so far as new capital goods are bought or old equipment sold for scrap, this is so. Such money is now 'active'. But in so far as such money is spent on existing capital goods in financing the capital loss arising from the reshuffle, such money is, in the Keynesian terminology, 'idle': its expenditure creates neither output nor employment, it merely facilitates the exchange of existing assets. Such money is therefore in every respect akin to money in the finan-

[8] 'In order that a complementary investment should be profitable, its cost must be less than the increase in the value of the old plant due to the complementary investment, that is, less than the value of the modernized or extended plant minus the value of the old plant. Thus, the more this latter value sinks, the more likely it is that complementary investment will pay' (Tord Palander: 'On the Concepts and Methods of the "Stockholm School"', *International Economic Papers*, vol. 3, p. 32).

cial circulation.   But if we follow Keynesian terminology, the
demand for idle money is governed by Liquidity Preference.
In our case, however, to say this would be absurd.   The size
of each firm's 'z', as we saw, depends not on its liquidity
preference but largely on what happens during the process of
exchange.   We saw that for some firms 'z' might actually be
negative.   The root of the trouble is that the Keynesian theory
of liquidity preference is a typical equilibrium theory with all
its limitations, and thus not very useful in cases of disequilibrium.   It tells us that a situation is conceivable in which
the relative marginal significance of each type of asset held
would be equal.   It demonstrates that such a situation would,
given our relative preferences for various assets, be preferable
to any other.   But it entirely fails to tell us how such a situation could ever be reached.   For in a dynamic world, while
the exchange of assets that might lead to an optimum position
is still going on, other changes will supervene which drastically
modify the situation.   In our case, for example, all attempts
to reach an 'optimum distribution' of assets were defeated by
the unexpected gains and losses which accompanied the
reshuffling of capital combinations, as a result of which some
firms found themselves with less, others with more money than
they had 'preferred'.   Any attempt at a reshuffle of assets in
the direction of 'optimum distribution' will set up those very
dynamic processes the results of which, had they been foreseen, would have induced the choice of another distribution.

We may now briefly summarize the conclusions we have
reached in this chapter.

In the first place, unexpected change, that chief vehicle of
all the more important economic processes, makes frequent
plan revisions necessary.   Such plan revisions involve changes
in existing capital combinations, i.e. regrouping decisions.

Secondly, decisions to regroup capital combinations, like
other plan revisions, involve the making of new plans.   The
decision to reshuffle is subject to the same hazards as other
plans: the reshuffle may fail.

Third, such failure of the regrouping plan will *inter alia*
result in a shift of the money holdings in various firms.   Hence,
such shifts must not be regarded as necessarily reflecting
'shifts in liquidity preference'.   Some of these shifts are among

the undesired consequences of plan revisions, decisions not made of free choice. The view that all shifts in money holdings reflect shifts in liquidity preference presents just another case where the essential characteristics of a dynamic process are assumed away by static assumptions.[9] Liquidity preference is seen to be essentially a static concept, inapplicable to a dynamic world.

Finally, we have seen that New Investment and Idle Capacity have also to be interpreted as the incidental results of dynamic processes. New investment depends primarily on the availability of cheap complementary resources of labour and capital. Their abundance is as often as not the result of dynamic processes of the past. Idle capacity is economically a form of scrap kept in physical existence by optimistic expectations of future value which may or may not be fulfilled. To understand why this capacity is kept in existence we need to understand, not merely why the original plans failed, but why no alternative use for it has been found.

All unexpected change causes capital gains and losses. These, far more than 'output', 'incomes', or even profits, are the real motor of a dynamic market economy. They are mostly the result of failure of production plans; but often the result of the failure of regrouping plans to materialize in accordance with a predetermined pattern.

[9] F. A. Hayek: *Individualism and Economic Order*, p. 94.

CHAPTER IV

THE MEANING OF CAPITAL STRUCTURE

In what follows we shall be concerned with the question what is meant by *capital structure*; in what circumstances it might exist or continue to exist; what forms it might take in varying circumstances; and what effects its changes or its disappearance would have on the economic system.

Structure implies function. Even in a building which consisted of stones completely alike these stones would have different functions. Those which support the outer walls have a function different from that of those which form floors and ceilings. In an important sense each stone supports all those above it. Physical homogeneity, we see, is not incompatible with functional difference. In every plan the instruments and materials used are always 'used together' in order to attain a given end; their functional difference determines the structure of their mode of use.

In the same way, all capital goods derive their economic significance from their mode of use, or rather, from their actual and potential modes of use. In this book we have rejected the conception of capital as a homogeneous aggregate. We realize that a heterogeneous capital concept compels us to seek the 'common denominator' of these heterogeneous resources, the common criterion of their capital quality, in their 'designed complementarity', their mode of use within the framework of a plan. Each plan is a logical structure in which means and ends are co-ordinated by a directing and controlling mind. In the functional variety which is of the very essence of capital utilization plans capital resources exhibit those *structural* relationships we shall have to study.

All capital goods are, directly or indirectly, instruments of production. Not all of them are man-made (e.g. mineral resources are not) but all of them are man-used. It is indeed characteristic of such 'natural' capital resources that but for the existence of man-made capital designed to be employed in conjunction with them, they would not even be economic goods.[1] The theory of capital is thus primarily a theory of the material instruments of production.[2] It must have something to say about the role of capital goods in production plans, about the mode of their combined use. In other words, production plans are the primary object of the theory of capital. In the first place, the theory deals with the way in which capital goods are used in plans, i.e. with the capital structure of production plans. In the second place, it also deals with the consistency of such plans within the economic system as a whole, i.e. with the *plan structure* of the economy. Since we are not interested in equilibrium (i.e. consistency) analysis for its own sake, our theory must also be able to deal with the more important cases of inconsistency of plans, and this means of disintegrating structures. In Chapter III we have had a glimpse of the consequences, for capital goods and their mode of use, of plan failure and plan revision. We must now, on a wider plane, apply this type of analysis to the consequences of capital regrouping for the economic system as a whole.

It follows from what has just been said that we have to distinguish between two types of capital complementarity: *plan complementarity*, the complementarity of capital goods within the framework of one plan, and *structural complementarity*, the over-all complementarity of capital goods within the economic system. The first type of complementarity is brought about *directly* by entrepreneurial action. The making and revision of such plans is the typical function of the entrepreneur.

Our second type of complementarity is, if at all, brought about *indirectly* by the market, viz. by the interplay of mostly inconsistent entrepreneurial plans. In Chapter III we have dealt with the first type of capital complementarity. In this chapter we shall be concerned with the second.

But it would be wrong to think of these two types of complementarity as the only possible forms of capital complementarity. The phenomenon of complementarity, of course,

[1] Cf. Carl Menger: *Principles of Economics* (transl. by James Dingwall and Bert F. Hoselitz), 1950, p. 155; and F. A. Hayek: *Pure Theory of Capital*, 1941, pp. 63–4.
[2] This is not to say that assets such as shares and bonds lie entirely beyond the scope of the theory of capital. But, as will be seen in Chapter VI, they are relevant for our purposes only in so far as their ownership does, or does not, influence the forces which determine where decision-making power, the power to make and revise production plans, lies.

extends as far as the realm of human plans and action. Wherever an action plan involves the use of specialized resources for whatever common purpose, complementarity is present. Complementarity is, in Professor Mises' terminology, a *praxeological category*. Within the narrower sphere of what is ordinarily regarded as economic action (*catallactic action*) other forms of capital complementarity can and do exist. In Chapter VI we shall learn that where action has to be taken in such a way as to safeguard the future control of productive resources without as yet making detailed plans for the future, there arises the complementarity of the Investment Portfolio which refers not to productive resources as such, but to the titles to their control, not to operating assets but to securities.

Before going on it may be helpful, for the sake of conceptual clarity, to compare and contrast the concept of Capital Complementarity, as it has so far emerged, with the concept of complementarity currently in use. According to Professor Hicks, who formulated this definition, 'Y is a substitute for X if the marginal rate of substitution of Y for money is diminished when X is substituted for money in such a way as to leave the consumer no better off than before. We must say that Y is complementary with X if the marginal rate of substitution of Y for money is increased when X is substituted for money.' (Italics in original.)[3]

For our purposes this is not a useful definition. The reason for this does not, as one might think at first, lie in the fact that the Hicksian definition originated in the sphere of consumption and was meant to be applied primarily to consumer goods, whereas we are here concerned with capital complementarity as a form of factor complementarity. The real reason for the inadequacy of the Hicksian definition for our purposes lies in the fact that the world of the consumer, on which it is modelled, is conceived as a static world of instantaneous adjustment, while the type of process analysis to which we are committed compels us to regard adjustment as essentially *discontinuous*. The increase in 'the marginal rate of substitution of Y for money when X is substituted for money' has to be regarded as an *instantaneous act* of the consumer, quite irrespective of anything he may have thought or done or

[3] J. R. Hicks: *Value and Capital*, 1939, p. 44.

planned before. It is, in effect, an immediate predictable 'response' to the situation confronting him. Nothing is said about the question why such a situation should arise, nor why the consumer should react in the manner postulated. No doubt the consumer had made a plan in accordance with which he acts. How did he make it? We are not told.

The fatal weakness of all mechanistic theories is that they must let human action appear 'determinate', if only by man's own plans, and are thus prevented from understanding the acts of the mind which constitute these plans. A theory without plans cannot grasp planned action. A definition of complementarity couched in terms of instantaneous substitution clearly does not fit into a world of intermittently fixed capital coefficients.

Our emphasis on factor complementarity does not imply of course that factor substitution is unimportant. When, at discontinuous intervals in the form of plan revision, substitution takes place, it is, as we saw in Chapter III, most important and often has far-reaching consequences. What matters to us, however, is that once we have introduced the distinction between planned action and plan revision, factors may be complements in one *and* substitutes in another situation. Suppose, for instance, that a store has four delivery vans, physically completely alike, each of which delivers goods in one quarter of the town. Are they complements or substitutes? Evidently, at the moment at which the production plan is made they are perfect substitutes for each other. But once the plan is set in motion they are turned into complements. If now one of them breaks down, the production plan for the whole town breaks down. The fact of the matter is that 'factor complementarity and substitution are phenomena belonging to different provinces of the realm of action. Complementarity is a property of means employed to the same end, or a group of consistent ends. All the means jointly employed for the same end, or such ends, are necessarily complements. In other words, factor complementarity requires a *plan* within the framework of which each factor has a function. It is therefore only with respect to a given plan that we can meaningfully speak of factor complementarity. Factors are complements in so far as they fit into a production plan and participate in a productive process.

'Substitution, on the other hand, is a phenomenon of change, the need for which arises whenever something has gone wrong with a prior plan. Factor substitution is a concomitant of plan revision, and can therefore only take place intermittently between our "periods". And substitutibility essentially indicates the ease with which a factor can be turned into an element of a plan.' [4]

We now have to face the central problem of this chapter. What do we mean by *capital structure*?

In the social sciences we mean by 'structure' a complex of relationships sufficiently stable in varying circumstances to display the firm outline of a clear and distinguishable pattern. Structural stability of such a complex thus does not require complete absence of external change impinging on it. It is true that the more violent the impact of such change, the less the pattern is likely to last. But as the social world is inevitably a world of unexpected change, any concept of stability applicable to it must refer to *internal coherence* in the face of external change rather than to absence of the latter. Consistency of the relationships which constitute the complex is thus of the essence of the matter. In economics, for instance, the static equilibrium concept of neo-classical economics means at bottom nothing more than this. It does not require a *stationary world* as its setting. If equilibrium means nothing more than consistency of a complex of relationships, it can be extended to the world of change if by 'dynamic equilibrium' we mean consistency of plans.

In the theory of capital we can thus easily speak of a structure as long as utilization plans succeed and capital goods stay where they are. But as soon as plans have to be revised and factor combinations reshuffled, a structure in this sense no longer exists. We might thus define *capital structure* negatively in terms of the absence of the regrouping of capital combinations. A capital structure, we might say, exists as long as the various capital goods remain neatly pigeon-holed in their respective capital combinations and are being replaced

[4] L. M. Lachmann: 'Complementarity and Substitution in the Theory of Capital', *Economica*, May 1947, p. 110.

by their replicas as they wear out. In other words, capital structure might be defined in terms of the constant composition of the capital combinations which form the material backbone of production plans. But this, of course, is an essentially static notion of capital structure. It is not incompatible with economic progress as long as we assume that progress takes preponderantly the form of new investment, that is to say, as long as we assume that new capital combinations take their place side by side with the existing ones without disturbing the latter. This, in fact, is how the Keynesians, Mr. Harrod and even Professor Hicks, conceive of economic progress. It is only when we realize that the distinction between *external* capital change in the form of investment (formation of new capital combinations) and *internal* capital change (regrouping) is entirely artificial and that one cannot take place without the other, that we come to doubt the usefulness of this notion of capital structure.

There is, however, another equally important reason why we cannot accept a definition of capital structure in terms of the constant composition of capital combinations. Not the individual capital goods but the service streams to which they give rise are the primary objects of our desires, and hence the ultimate determinants of the economic system. Capital goods are merely the *nodal points* of the flows of input (of labour and other capital services) which they absorb, and of output (of intermediate or final products) which they emanate. The same capital good may give rise to service streams of very different kind. The same building may be used as a cotton mill or a toy factory, the same ship carry a cargo of coal or of bananas. Now, where a plant is switched over to the production of a different output stream, even although the capital combination of which it forms part need not undergo change, it will almost certainly affect the success of the production plans of those from whom it buys and to whom it sells. If so, the production change mentioned will make necessary the reshuffling of other capital combinations. Moreover, it is unlikely that a capital good can be turned over to another use without affecting its own mode of combination with other factors of production. Hence, there will have to be regrouping in the firm which starts the change as well as in those which are affected by it.

If this is so, what remains of our concept of the capital structure? Of course we can imagine, if we care to, a completely *stationary* (as distinct from *static*) world in which, year in year out, the same service streams flow into and out of each capital combination, and the same final products are dutifully swallowed by consumers. We could then have a capital structure defined not merely in terms of the constant composition of capital combinations but also of service streams. But what good would it do? The price of simplification is aridity. Such a conception would be quite inapplicable to a world of processes and change.

The result of our examination of the notion of capital structure thus appears to be that in dynamic reality there can be no such thing. If this were really so, it would entail grave consequences for the theory of capital and its application to actual problems. A morphological theory of capital such as ours, couched in terms of the heterogeneous resources we observe in reality, cannot do without a central concept which reduces chaos to order and indicates the pattern of that order. And what form other than that of structure could such a coherent pattern have?

Nor would the consequences be less grave if we attempted to apply our theory of capital. For instance, in Chapter VII we shall speak of 'intersectional maladjustments' as a feature of industrial fluctuations. Without a concept of structure as the norm from which all maladjustments can be regarded as deviations such a notion evidently can make no sense.

Confronted with the dilemma that in the theory of capital we cannot do without a central concept, but can find no such concept as could stand up to unexpected change, it seems that we must go back to fundamentals. A structure is a complex of relationships which exhibit a coherent pattern. The relationships exist between *entities*. It is probable that when these entities undergo change, so will the relationships between them: probable but not necessary. We may imagine the entities changing in such a fashion that the complex of relationships between them remains unchanged; as ships in convoy may keep the same distance whether they sail in the North Sea or in the Caribbean, whether they carry a cargo of iron ore or of wool. In modern economics the notion of *intertemporal or dynamic* equilibrium is a good example: 'This sort of fictitious state of equilibrium which (irrespective of whether there is any reason to believe that it will actually come about) can be *conceived* to comprise any sort of planned change, is indispensable if we want to apply the technique of equilibrium analysis at all to phenomena which are *ex definitione* absent in a stationary state. It is in this sphere alone that we can usefully discuss equilibrium relations extending over time.' [5]

We have here 'the case where these plans are fully adjusted to one another, so that it is possible for all of them to be carried out because the plans of any one member are based on the expectation of such actions on the part of the other members as are contained in the plans which those others are making at the same time. This is clearly the case where people know exactly what is going to happen for the reason that the same operations have been repeated time after time over a very long period. But the concept as such can also be applied to situations which are not stationary and where the same correspondence between plans prevails, not because people just continue to do what they have been doing in the past, *but because they correctly foresee what changes will occur* in the actions of others.' [6]

We shall distinguish between cases of *consistent* and *inconsistent* capital change. By *structural maladjustment* we shall mean inconsistent capital change, change which affects the flow of service streams from one capital combination to another, from production stage to production stage, in such a way as to deflect these streams from their expected courses, frustrating the expectations of those who had made preparations to receive the service streams in their particular 'receptacles', i.e. factor combinations, and, when transformed, to release them again.

Of consistent capital change, on the other hand, we may speak where 'coincident expectations about the quantities and qualities of goods which will pass from one person's possession into another's will in effect co-ordinate all these different plans into one single plan, although this "plan" will not exist in any one mind. It can only be constructed.' [7]

[5] F. A. Hayek: *Pure Theory of Capital*, 1941, pp. 18–19.
[6] F. A. Hayek, op. cit., p. 18.   [7] Ibid., p. 26.

In reality, of course, such a state of coincident expectations could scarcely exist, at least in an industrial society in which the division of labour has evolved to any noticeable extent. But this does not mean that economic forces tending to make expectations consistent with each other ('stabilizers') do not exist here. It merely means that such forces do not operate in a vacuum, that often they meet with obstacles and sometimes with counterforces tending to deflect them from their courses. Sheer stubborn ignorance and unwillingness to learn on the part of some producers or consumers may be such an obstacle. But a more frequent form of obstacle is to be found in institutional prohibitions of the full use of whatever knowledge is already available, for instance in certain forms of the Patent Law.

We may also note that within a given economic system there may operate at the same time a number of what we may call 'partially co-ordinating forces' which, while each is calculated to integrate whatever part of the system is within its reach, in effect obstruct each other and tend to create general chaos. Most of the so-called 'market stabilization' schemes which were so popular in the 1930's, as well as attempts to conceal the effects of malinvestment at one stage of production by means of 'vertical integration', are examples of it. Another example, perhaps better known and more widely discussed, is the destructive effect of national 'planning' policies on the world economy. By contrast, whatever degree of the international division of labour there still exists in the world is the result of competition, the individual pursuit of unconcerted and therefore initially by no means necessarily consistent plans. The complementarity of factors of production employed in primary producing and manufacturing countries and in international transport is the cumulative result of a continuous succession of substitutions. Thus continuous substitution serves to promote universal factor complementarity.

Our next task is to assess the strength and describe the *modus operandi* of those forces which in a market economy bring expectations into consistency with each other, stabilize economic relationships, and integrate the economic system as a whole. Foremost among these forces is *the price system*.

In a market economy, as we pointed out in Chapter II, prices are not merely exchange ratios between commodities and services but links in a market-wide system of economic communications. Through price changes knowledge is transmitted from any corner of any market to the rest of the system. On each market buyers and sellers, by varying their bids and offers, signal to each other the need for action. Buyers learn about their opportunities growing or shrinking, sellers receive notice of the need for adjustment. In this way every economic change has its market-wide repercussions. Suppose that an engineering firm finds a method of substituting a cheaper metal for a more expensive one in one of its products. The lower price of the metal thus far used will notify producers that they must look for other outlets, the higher price of the new metal asks its producers to increase supply. If the price of the engineering product is not reduced, high profits made will tell potential competitors where their opportunity lies; if price is reduced the public comes to know of its new opportunity. Similarly we can trace the effect on complementary factors and competing products. We may thus conclude that via knowledge transmitted through the price system economic change tends, in general, to give rise to expectations consistent with itself.

But in reality the price system is not such an ideal system of economic communications as the picture just drawn might suggest. Our apparatus, we must remember, works by 'translating' demand and supply changes into price changes. Hence, whenever the translation does not take place, for instance, where prices are inflexible, our apparatus ceases to operate. Moreover, as we learnt before, transmission is often delayed and sometimes faulty. Where this is known to be the case the meaning of the messages received will lend itself to different, and perhaps contrasting, interpretations, both as to content and time of despatch. This all the more so where numerous, perhaps contradictory, messages follow each other within a short time over the same 'wire'. In general we may say that in a market economy repeated inconsistent action is likely to be either the result of price inflexibility or of 'functionless' price movements. Such movements will be functionless where, for instance, there is a long delay in transmission, and in particular where the delay is different for different markets so that at the moment of receipt of the messages it becomes impossible to reconstruct the chronological order in which the events to which they give expression actually occurred. Where simultaneous changes of data are not reflected by simultaneous price changes action based on prices will be either premature or delayed.[8]

There can be little doubt that in modern industrial society *price inflexibility* is a prominent phenomenon, and that it is likely to be on the increase. In the economic literature of the 1930's the phenomenon has often been linked with the 'growth of monopoly'. Mr. Paul Sweezy explained it as a feature of oligopoly.[9] But the association of rigid prices with monopoly has been subjected to severe criticism by Professor Scitovszky[10] who showed that, on purely theoretical grounds, monopolists confronted with shifting inelastic demand curves would have no reason to keep their prices stable. More recently, Mr. Streeten[11] has cast doubt on the applicability of the whole mechanism of equilibrium theory to the problem complex of price-output decisions in a situation in which producers know that their acts will have ulterior consequences on those of others (expectations being here, as so often in modern theory, the villain in the piece), and demand curves no longer have a clear meaning.

We believe that these somewhat unsatisfactory conclusions are the result of a failure to grasp the nature of the market as a vehicle for the transmission of knowledge, and of the vain attempt to analyse market processes in terms of equilibrium analysis, that is, to regard every market situation as a 'state of rest' instead of as a transitional stage of a continuous process.

It seems to us that we need to look at the whole problem in its historical setting. Inflexible prices characterize a market

---

[8] These, of course, are the cases in which the significance of price movements has to be judged with the help of supplementary criteria, like the time factor and the size and variations of stocks. Cf. above, pp. 31–2.

[9] P. M. Sweezy: 'Demand under Conditions of Oligopoly', *Journal of Political Economy*, August 1939, pp. 568–73.

[10] T. de Scitovszky: 'Prices under Monopoly and Competition', *Journal of Political Economy*, October 1941.

[11] P. Streeten: 'Reserve Capacity and the Kinked Demand Curve', *Review of Econ. Studies*, Vol. XVIII, No. 2, pp. 103–14.

situation in which the transmission of knowledge from buyers to sellers and vice versa is at least temporarily impeded. Rigid prices are 'administered' prices in a situation in which the 'administrators' regard the knowledge they can withhold (from buyers and competitors) as more valuable than the knowledge they might gain by experimenting with price variations. 'Fear of spoiling the market' is essentially fear of what consumers and competitors will do in the future with the knowledge derived from price change now.

Historically speaking, the most important cause of price rigidity has been the decline of the wholesale merchant.[12] Here was a broker whose interest was primarily in maximizing turnover, and who could therefore be relied upon to offer manufacturers and charge retailers such prices as would enable him to accomplish this aim. Here was an ideal vehicle for the transmission of knowledge, since, unlike the consumer who spends his income on a large variety of goods and services and cannot afford to acquire expert information on each, it paid the wholesale merchant (in fact it was a condition of his economic survival) to acquire the latest information about alternative sources of supply and their respective qualities, and to make use of it. Here, in short, was a 'middleman' whose economic function was not so much to 'distribute goods' as to collect and impart information and to fix such prices as would maximize his turnover. And such prices evidently had to be flexible!

This is not the place to discuss the reasons for the decline of the wholesale merchant. We are not writing economic history, but merely endeavour to use historical facts to illustrate a theoretical argument. One reason for his decline is clearly the standardization of many products of modern industry. Those economists who are in the habit of denouncing product differentiation as one of the 'wastes of competition' and who extol standardization as the hallmark of efficiency, will welcome the decline of the wholesale merchant. They tell us that 'distribution costs too much'. But their argument

---

[12] The argument which follows in the text draws heavily upon certain ideas set forth by R. G. Hawtrey: *The Economic Problem*, pp. 19–23 and 34–43, and N. Kaldor: 'The Economic Aspects of Advertising', *Review of Econ. Studies*, Vol. XVIII, No. 1, pp. 16–18. Neither of these two authors must be held responsible for what we say in the text.

appears to depend on the curious assumption that progress has come to an end, that all possible methods of production and their relative merits are already known today to everybody concerned, and that no further knowledge is to be gained by product differentiation, experiment, and market observation. In other words, these economists are really assuming that we are living in a stationary state! Others will doubt whether in a world of unexpected change the gains from standardization will in all cases outweigh the social loss caused by the disappearance of an economic agent capable of, and interested in, testing the market at frequent intervals. There are 'economies' which cost too much.

We saw in Chapter II that even where all prices are flexible all price movements are not equally significant in spreading knowledge, and that there are always some price movements which are functionless. In order to cope with this problem we introduced in Chapter II, following Dr. Lange, the concept of the Practical Range which we divided into an inner and an outer range. We found that this concept can be used in such a way as to permit us to draw a distinction between price phenomena which are consistent with the existing structure of expectations, fall 'within the ranges', and thus cause no disappointment, and, on the other hand, phenomena inconsistent with the existing structure of expectations, which fall 'outside the ranges' a revision of which they necessitate.[13]

Functionless price movements are thus those which, confined to within the inner ranges, can cast no doubt and thus throw no light on the feasibility of plans. Hence they convey no new information. It is only when prices cross the limits of the ranges that the 'alarm bell rings'. Then at least those plans in which the respective price estimates played an important part will require revision.

In Chapter II we confined our analysis of the interaction of price change and expectations to a single market. We shall now extend it to price relationships between a number of markets.

All entrepreneurial action, viz. the making and revision of plans, is governed by expected profits. Profits depend on prices and costs. Where all relevant costs and prices rise

[13] See above, p. 33.

pari passu (as in the classical theory of inflation) profitability remains unaffected. If, for instance, all costs and prices relevant to a given plan cross the upper limits of inner and outer ranges at the same moment, their effects neutralize each other. Where all the alarm bells ring at the same moment, those telling of gain as well as those telling of loss, no plan revision would be called for.

But in reality this is of course not likely to happen. Prices and costs are not equally flexible, where flexible do not move at equal rates, and even if they did, their outer and inner ranges would prove to be of unequal magnitude. We therefore find that for instance in an inflation all bells will not ring at the same time, and the fictitious intervals thus convey misleading information: the plans will look more successful than they actually are. Expansion programmes prompted by fictitious profits will be started which would not have been started if the inevitable subsequent rise in costs had been foreseen. Thus there is Malinvestment, the waste of capital resources in plans prompted by misleading information.

For some enterprises, to be sure, the profits may be 'real' enough. For instance, a young and heavily indebted industry may be able to pay off part of its debt out of such paper profits. But the 'knowledge' thus spread is none the less fictitious and action based on it must lead to failure. Others will react to these events by investing capital in the industry which later on will be lost. This is one, though probably the most important, case of inconsistent capital change. The effect of such misguided investment on incomes and employment will be discussed in detail in Chapter VII. There we shall see that at least one kind of industrial fluctuation has its chief cause in inconsistent capital change due to partial failure of the price mechanism.

We have seen that the integrating forces of the price system, tending to bring expectations and the plans based on them into consistency with each other, do not operate unimpeded. There are counterforces among which Price Inflexibility, the force of economic inertia, is perhaps the most notable. But even where this force is eventually overcome, it will not be overcome everywhere at the same moment. Time intervals arise which by robbing some of the price messages of their original meaning create problems of their own. Behind them all there lurks ultimately the problem of interpretation. For in our communications system there does not exist a clear and definite code which would permit us to find the 'factual content' of the messages. Some of them are meaningless, others are not. And each message, as we saw, makes sense only within a given frame of reference, a framework of plans largely governed by the structure of expectations.

It is only when held against what they were expected to be, that the 'facts of a situation' begin to tell a story. In the whole field of human action, and therefore also in the sciences studying it, observation without interpretation is futile. All interpretation requires a pre-existent structure of thought to serve as a frame of reference.

It would be wrong to think that a market economy, when faced with the problems just outlined, could, or in the ordinary course of events would, find no answer to them. History shows that whenever left sufficiently free from political interference to evolve its responses to such challenges, the market economy has 'grown' the institutions necessary to deal with them. In particular, it has evolved institutions to protect the integrating forces of the price system from the disintegrating forces just described. Among these institutions *forward markets* and the *Stock Exchange* call for our particular attention.

In saying that the market economy, for speed of adjustment and, in general, operational efficiency, depends on the price system as a network of communications, we have thus far assumed that the content of the messages transmitted refers to events that have actually 'happened', i.e. to events of the past. But this need not be so. It is precisely the economic function of forward markets to spread knowledge not about what is or has been, but about what people think will be. In this way, while the future will always remain uncertain, it is possible for the individual to acquire knowledge about other people's expectations and to adjust his own accordingly, expressing his own views about future prices by buying or selling forward, thus adding his own mite to the formation of market opinion as expressed in forward prices. In other words, forward markets tend to bring expectations into consistency with each other.[14] They are on the side of the stabilizers.

In reality forward trading is usually limited to a small number of commodities, and even trading in these is as a rule confined to a few future dates (three months, six months, twelve months ahead). The *Stock Exchange*, on the other hand, offers an instance of trading in 'continuous futures'. If I buy a share I buy not merely this year's dividend and next year's dividend but, in principle, an infinite and continuous series of dividends, a 'yield stream'. In buying it I thus express explicitly a series of expectations about dividends, and implicitly an expectation about the future yield from other assets I might have bought instead. To the extent to which my action has an effect on the price of the share, and unless of course this effect is offset by somebody else's sale at the *former* price, the series of my expectations becomes manifest in the price change. Every purchase or sale which modifies a price conveys to the market knowledge about somebody's expectations. If the directors of a company announce a bold expansion programme, the effect of their announcement on the price of their shares tells them whether or not the market agrees with their expectations: If price falls it means that the market takes a less optimistic view of the company's prospects, and such a price fall will convey a warning signal to the directors that they must walk warily.

The Stock Exchange is a market in 'continuous futures'. It has therefore always been regarded by economists as the central market of the economic system and a most valuable economic barometer, a market, that is, which in its relative valuation of the various yield streams reflects, in a suitably 'objectified' form, the articulate expectations of all those who wish to express them. All this may sound rather platitudinous and might hardly be worth mentioning were it not for the fact that it differs from the Keynesian theory of the Stock Exchange which is now so much *en vogue*.

In order to defend our own view it is therefore necessary to enter upon a critical discussion of the Keynesian view of the economic function of the Stock Exchange. This view is

[14] J. R. Hicks: *Value and Capital*, pp. 135–40, and J. K. Eastham: *An Introduction to Economic Analysis*, 1950, pp. 162–4.

summed up in the famous sentence, 'When the capital development of a country becomes a by-product of the activities of a casino, the job is likely to be ill-done.'[15] How did Keynes arrive at this conclusion?

The marginal efficiency of capital is one of the main pillars of the Keynesian edifice. It is defined in terms of prospective yield and supply price of capital assets. The latter, we are explicitly told, is 'not the market price at which an asset of the type in question can actually be purchased in the market',[16] but the cost of a newly produced asset.

Stock Exchange prices of 'existing assets' thus seem to be excluded from the scope of the definition. Later on, however, we are told that 'a high quotation for existing equities *involves* (our italics) an increase in the marginal efficiency of the corresponding type of capital'.[17] Whether or not this conflicts with the earlier definition depends on our interpretation of the word 'involves'. This could probably be interpreted to mean no more than 'has an influence on', the vehicle of this influence having to be sought in 'prospective yield'.[18]

But this point of consistency in the definition of investment is perhaps of minor significance. Far more important is Keynes' attitude to the fundamental question: Is the Stock Exchange a suitable instrument for bringing long-term expectations into consistency; is it capable of giving rise to a, socially 'objectified', *market opinion* to guide investment decisions? Here Keynes' answer is a clear and unqualified 'No'. 'For most of these persons are, in fact, largely concerned, not with making superior long-term forecasts of the probable yield of an investment over its whole life, but with foreseeing changes in the conventional basis of valuation a short time ahead of the general public.'[19] This is 'an inevitable result of an investment market organized along the lines described. For it is not sensible to pay 25 for an investment of which you believe the

[15] J. M. Keynes: *General Theory of Employment*, p. 159.
[16] Ibid., p. 135.   [17] Ibid., p. 151, n. 1.
[18] Mrs. Robinson says that 'Keynes creates confusion by calling ordinary shares "real assets", and describing the purchase of shares on the Stock Exchange as an act of investment' (*The Rate of Interest*, p. 7, n. 1). We doubt whether the charge of confusion can be sustained. By using the words 'corresponding type of capital' in the passage quoted above Keynes appears to have drawn the relevant distinction.
[19] Ibid., p. 154.

F

prospective yield to justify a value of 30, if you also believe that the market will value it at 20 three months hence.'[20]

It is readily seen that the defect criticized by Keynes is not a defect of investment markets as such, but a defect of investment markets without a provision for forward trading. Where forward trading exists, a person holding the views described could express his short-term view by selling the investment at any price above 20 for three months ahead, while expressing his long-term view by buying it, say, 18 months forward at a price below 30. If everybody did it arbitrage would do the rest by bringing the forward prices for various future dates into line with each other. Price expectations involve intertemporal price relations, and intertemporal price relations cannot be made explicit, hence cannot be adequately expressed, without an intertemporal market. All we can conclude from Keynes' argument is not that the Stock Exchange cannot make yield expectations consistent, but that without forward trading it cannot do so.

But this is not all. Keynes not merely failed to realize the real nature of the specific problem he was facing, viz. intertemporal price inconsistency expressing itself in divergent expectations. He was probably unaware of the importance, perhaps even of the existence, of the class of problems of which this is one: problems of the transmission of knowledge. There is very little evidence that he grasped the economic function of the market as an institution through which people exchange knowledge with each other. The Keynesian world is a world in which there are two distinct classes of actors: the skilled investor, 'who, unperturbed by the prevailing pastime, continues to purchase investments on the best genuine long-term expectations he can frame';[21] and, on the other hand, the ignorant 'game-player'. It does not seem to have occurred to Keynes that either of these two may learn from the other, and that, in particular, company directors and even the managers of investment trusts may be the wiser for learning from the market what it thinks about their actions. In this Keynesian world the managers and directors already know all about the future and have little to gain from devoting their attention to

[20] J. M. Keynes: *General Theory of Employment*, p. 155.
[21] Ibid., p. 156.

the *misera plebs* of the market. In fact, Keynes strongly feels that they should not! This pseudo-Platonic view of the world of high finance forms, we feel, an essential part of what Schumpeter called the 'Keynesian vision'. This view ignores progress through exchange of knowledge because the ones know already all there is to be known whilst the others never learn anything. The view stands in clear and irreconcilable contrast to the view of the role of knowledge in society we have consistently endeavoured to set forth in this book. The reader will not be surprised to learn that our conclusions on the subject of the Stock Exchange are equally irreconcilable with those of Keynes.

We hold that the Stock Exchange by facilitating the exchange of knowledge tends to make the expectations of large numbers of people consistent with each other, at least more consistent than they would have been otherwise; and that through the continual revaluation of yield streams it promotes *consistent capital change* and therefore economic progress. This, of course, is not to say that the Stock Exchange makes inconsistent capital change impossible: merely, that company directors who ignore the signals of the market do so at their peril, and that in the long run a market economy substitutes entrepreneurs who can read the signs of the times for those who cannot.

CHAPTER V

CAPITAL STRUCTURE
AND ECONOMIC PROGRESS

In Chapter III we saw how entrepreneurs form and dissolve capital combinations in response to the varying needs of changing situations, and how these capital combinations, embodied in plans, have to be regarded at each moment as the 'atoms' of the capital structure. In Chapter IV we endeavoured to show how the forces inherent in a market economy tend to operate towards consistent capital change and a coherent pattern of service streams flowing into and out of capital combinations; and that in this sense we may say that a *capital structure*, though it could hardly ever exist for any length of time, is always in the process of being formed, a process continually interrupted by unexpected change. In this chapter we shall be chiefly concerned with the changes which the capital structure undergoes as capital is accumulated or, as we might say, with the specific forms the capital structure assumes in an 'expanding economy'.

In Chapter III we thus saw how the ultimate constituents are determined, in Chapter IV how these constituents tend to form a system. In the present chapter we shall study the properties of this system under conditions of 'uniform' change.

We shall, however, have to change our method of attack. Thus far we have built up our argument, by and large, by the analysis and interpretation of certain well-known facts of business life, paying scant attention to what economic theories have to say about them; taking our justification for such disregard from the fact that theorists have, on the whole, had little to say about the matters in which we are interested, and that what little they have to say is, like Keynes' theory of speculation, as often as not misleading rather than to the point.

In other words, it is of the nature of our approach that we are looking at capital as the entrepreneur does, who has to build up capital combinations from a diversity of material resources. So we had little to learn from economists who adopt the point of view of the accountant, private or social, to whom the common denominator of the capital account is the heart of the matter, and most economists have at least implicitly adopted the accountant's point of view. But we shall now have to deal with one of the exceptions. In studying changes in the capital structure we cannot ignore previous discussions.

We shall in this chapter be mainly concerned with a question to which the intuitive genius of Boehm-Bawerk gave an answer of a kind, an answer, to be sure, we cannot fully accept and which, moreover, is marred by an excessive degree of simplification, yet an answer we cannot afford to disregard.

We ask what typical changes the capital structure undergoes as capital is accumulated. Boehm-Bawerk's answer was, briefly, that the 'period of production' increases and causes an increase in output per man-hour. We cannot accept this answer as it stands, but we believe it possible to re-interpret it in such a way as to make it exempt from most of the more damaging attacks it has suffered in recent years. Our procedure in this chapter will therefore take the form of a re-interpretation of Boehm-Bawerk's thesis about the higher productivity of 'Roundabout Production'.

There is a certain inconsistency in Boehm-Bawerk's theory which is relevant to our purpose in this chapter, and to which we must turn first. On the one hand, no other economist saw more clearly than he the essential heterogeneity of all capital. He speaks of capital as a 'mass of intermediate products' or a 'complex of products destined for further production'. On the other hand, his theory is essentially an attempt to reduce this 'complex' to a common denominator and to measure all changes in it in the single dimension of time. It seems to us that the root of his failure lies in this inconsistency. Starting from a view of the capital problem which is fundamentally sound, he failed when he tried to introduce the incongruous element of single-dimension measurement into a theory conceived in terms of heterogeneous products.

In re-interpreting Boehm-Bawerk it will be our task to separate what is relevant to our purpose from much that is not. For Boehm-Bawerk of course the 'higher productivity of roundabout production' was important merely as the 'third ground' for the explanation of the existence of the rate of

interest.   As we pointed out in Chapter I, we are not interested
in interest as such.   Why a (positive) rate of interest exists,
is a question which does not concern us directly in our quest
for the forces which shape. the capital structure.   But indirectly it does concern us.

After all, men invest capital in order to have an income.
They reshuffle capital goods in order to obtain a higher income
than they otherwise would.   All capital change is governed
by the magnitude of the income thus obtained—and this
income is interest!

It is impossible to strip an argument of irrelevancies without
considering what they are, or at least might be, relevant to.
Our contention in what follows will be that Boehm-Bawerk's
'third ground' is an important element of the theory of economic progress which somehow, by mistake, its author put into
the wrong pigeonhole and inserted into his theory of interest.
The nature of this mistake will have to be elucidated.   And
the first step in this elucidation will have to consist in showing
that the rate of interest can be 'explained' without the help
of his 'third ground'.   To this task we now have to turn,
and in doing so we must for a little while digress from our
main path.   No originality is claimed for what we shall have
to say in this digression.   In showing that a positive rate of
interest would exist even in a stationary economy we simply
follow the implications of the argument so lucidly set forth
by Professor Lindahl.[1]   We shall then attempt to show that
the validity of the argument is not impaired by recent 'monetary' doctrines of the interest rate as long as the difference
between equilibrium conditions and the equilibrating mechanism is firmly kept in mind.

Of late a controversy has raged in the field of the theory of
interest on whether the rate of interest is a 'real' or a 'purely
monetary' phenomenon.   The former may be called the
'traditional' view of the matter, while the latter, though by
no means entirely new, derives most of its present-day im-
petus from Keynes.   We shall see that once we distinguish
clearly between equilibrium and disequilibrium conditions,
and take the trouble to define the circumstances in which

[1] *Studies in the Theory of Money and Capital*, pp. 288–91.

intertemporal equilibrium is at all conceivable, the substance of the controversy vanishes.[2]

The rate of interest is the overall rate of exchange of present for future goods. It is thus an intertemporal exchange rate. There will be as many intertemporal exchange rates as there are future dates at which goods will become available, just as there are as many international exchange rates as there are countries participating in international trade. Just as these 'foreign exchange rates' require a 'foreign exchange market' to become explicit and to reach an equilibrium level, so intertemporal exchange rates must be settled in an *intertemporal market*. To understand the phenomenon at all we must assume forward markets for tin, copper, houses, etc., in which the 'own-rates' of interest are fixed for three months, six months, a year, etc.

It is readily seen that these 'own-rates' will tend to become equal if we allow for differences in the cost of carrying stocks. Arbitrage will bring this about. Let us first assume a barter economy with forward markets for each commodity and no cost of carrying stock. If a present house sells for 100 tons of 'spot' copper, and a house available a year hence for 100 tons of twelve months' forward copper, and the 'own-rate' for both copper and houses is 10 per cent, then the house available a year hence must sell for 90 tons of 'spot' copper. If the price were either more or less than 90 tons, i.e. if the own-rate for houses were either higher or lower than that for copper, 'switching' would take place. The good with the lower own-rate would be sold, and its spot price would fall until the own-rates become equal. It is in our understanding this over-all rate of exchange of present for future goods, as it would establish itself in a barter economy, with an intertemporal market for most goods, which Wicksell had in mind when he spoke of 'the natural rate of interest'.

Let us now drop our two assumptions. If we allow for differences in the cost of carrying stocks we shall have different 'gross' own-rates, but the equilibrium relationship between

[2] The reader will not fail to notice that in the text we make an attempt to reconcile what we may call the 'neo-Wicksellian' theory of interest with the argument of Chapter 17 in Keynes' *General Theory* on 'The Essential Properties of Interest and Money', pp. 222–44. See also A. P. Lermer: 'The Essential Properties of Interest and Money', *Essays in Economic Analysis*, pp. 354–85.

own-rates remains; the own-rates *net of carrying cost* must still tend towards equality. The case is exactly parallel to the over-all equilibrium in the forward exchange market which subsists despite differences in interest rates in different financial centres which will make the 'swap' rates vary, but do not affect the net raté of profit.

Nor does the introduction of money with an intertemporal market to determine the money rate of interest affect our argument. The money rate of interest will have to adjust itself to the over-all commodity rate of intertemporal exchange. If, to start with, it is lower than the commodity rate (the familiar case of inflation) there will be a general 'switching' from money to goods, a 'flight from money' resulting in higher spot prices of goods in terms of present money and lower prices of future goods in terms of future money, until the commodity rate has fallen and the money rate, owing to the depletion of idle money stocks due to the 'flight' from it, has risen. *Vice versa* for the case in which the money rate exceeds the commodity rate: falling spot prices, rising forward prices, and an accumulating stock of 'idle' money would bring about the equality of the rates. The money rate no more 'rules the roost' than any other rate of intertemporal exchange.

Mr. Sraffa in 1932 was, to our knowledge, the first to point out that in this whole field the crucial distinction is between equilibrium and disequilibrium, and not between a barter economy and a money economy.[3] He developed the notion of own-rates, without actually coining the word, in an appropriate setting of forward markets, though unfortunately he considered these in isolation and thus failed to realize how, in a system of intertemporal markets, the market forces tend to re-establish equilibrium once it has been disturbed. He came to interpret Wicksell's 'natural rate' as an average of 'actual' own-rates as they would exist, side by side, in a barter

[3] 'Dr. Hayek on Money and Capital', *Economic Journal*, March 1932, p. 49. 'If money did not exist and loans were made in terms of all sorts of commodities, there would be a single rate which satisfies the conditions of equilibrium, but there might be at any moment as many "natural" rates of interest as there are commodities, though they would not be "equilibrium" rates. The "arbitrary" action of the banks is by no means a necessary condition for the divergence.'
Evidently Mr. Sraffa failed to see how in a barter economy intertemporal arbitrage would tend to bring the various 'natural' rates into conformity, thus tending towards establishing the 'equilibrium' rate.

economy,[4] and not as the result of the operation of market forces.   He thus substituted a statistical device for an analysis of market relationships.

In Keynes' system, by contrast, an over-all commodity rate does exist: the marginal efficiency of capital.   It is a peculiar feature of his teaching that when the marginal efficiency of capital exceeds the money rate of interest, equality is brought about by the market through investment, while when it falls short of it, disinvestment is the only equilibrating force.   This of course is due to his peculiar assumptions, first, that present prices, kept rigid by rigid wage-rates, cannot fall sufficiently to make investment profitable in the face of a high money rate, and, secondly, that accumulating money stocks have no effect on forward commodity prices.

When we abandon these restrictive assumptions we realize that there is a number of ways in which intertemporal market forces tend to bring the commodity rates and the money rate to equality; that investment is not the only *modus operandi* of these forces which would operate even in a stationary economy, i.e. one without investment; and that therefore the view of the rate of interest as an over-all intertemporal rate of exchange is not really affected by the Keynesian argument. It remains a curious fact, however, that Keynes, by making the distinction between the marginal efficiency of capital and the rate of interest the corner-stone of his system, actually re-enthroned that distinction between money and commodity rates for the irrelevance of which Wicksell and Professor Hayek had been so severely criticized by Mr. Sraffa, his acknowledged intellectual mentor in this matter.

There is one question which remains to be asked and answered by a theory of interest.   Can the rate of interest become negative?   Experience suggests that it cannot.   A theory of interest should be able to provide plausible general reasons to account for the fact that we only observe positive values of the phenomenon.

We know already why the money rate of interest cannot become negative while commodity rates remain positive: there would be a general 'switching' from money to goods, from loans to shares.   Very little money would be lent while the

4 Ibid., p. 51.

demand for loans would become immense. Who would not
become an entrepreneur if his creditors were ready to pay him
for it? The resulting excess demand for money loans would
soon bring back the rate of interest into the positive range.

So far we have merely demonstrated that the money rate
cannot, for any significant period, differ from the over-all
commodity rate, but we have not shown that the latter cannot
turn negative. Yet it is readily seen that it cannot. The ultimate reason for this lies in the simple fact that stocks of goods
can be carried forward in time, but not backwards. If
present prices of future goods are higher than those of present
goods, it is possible to convert the latter into the former unless
the good is perishable or the cost of storing excessive; while
future goods cannot be converted into present goods unless
there are ample stocks not otherwise needed which their
holders are ready to reduce for a consideration. And as there
are always a number of goods for which the cost of storage
would be small, money being one of them, a negative rate
of interest would be eliminated by a high demand for present
goods which are easy to store and a large supply of easily
storable future goods, at least as long as the stocks carried
are covered by forward sales.

We now have to return to our chief task in this chapter, the
re-examination of Boehm-Bawerk's third ground. We have
just seen that the phenomenon of the rate of interest can be
adequately accounted for without it; that a positive rate of
interest would exist even under stationary conditions which
do not, of course, preclude the intertemporal transfer of goods
any more than they preclude the inter-local transfer of goods,
but only preclude unexpected change, and that means change
in knowledge. Boehm-Bawerk's third ground is thus not a
necessary condition of the existence of interest. But what is
its true role? In Professor Lindahl's words, 'Although the
third ground is therefore not a necessary condition for the
existence of a rate of interest on capital, it is actually of the
most decisive importance for the concrete level of the interest
rate, as a determining factor on the demand side.'[5] How does
it have this effect?

[5] Lindahl, op. cit., p. 291.

First of all, we must try to see Boehm-Bawerk's thesis in its proper setting. Like Adam Smith's Division of Labour to which, as we shall see presently, it is closely related, the principle of roundabout production is, correctly interpreted, a theorem about economic progress. Now, the full significance of a theorem in any science can only be shown under 'artificial' conditions requiring a higher or lower level of abstraction. These make up 'the world' in which the theorem would be true.

It so happens that the world of Boehm-Bawerk, as the world of Adam Smith, differs from the conceptual systems familiar to economists of the mid-twentieth century: it is neither a stationary nor a fully dynamic world. In a stationary world of course there can be no capital investment; while of the disconcertingly dynamic world of our daily experience technical progress is an outstanding feature. As Boehm-Bawerk often pointed out, roundaboutness is not a form of technical progress. Technical progress requires new forms of knowledge spreading through the economic system while Boehm-Bawerk assumes a given knowledge equally shared by all. The world of Boehm-Bawerk is, then, a peculiar world of restricted progress, of progress in only one direction: that of capital accumulation the results of which are predictable. In this respect it is quite similar to the recent models of Messrs. Harrod and Hicks who have adopted Cassel's notion of the 'uniformly progressive economy' without unexpected change and have saved their models from the effects of the more disconcerting features of progress by the simple assumption of a 'steady rate of progress'.

For Adam Smith the division of labour was the most important source of progress. The same principle can be applied to capital. As capital accumulates there takes place a 'division of capital', a specialization of individual capital items, which enables us to resist the law of diminishing returns. As capital becomes more plentiful its accumulation does not take the form of multiplication of existing items, but that of a change in the composition of capital combinations. Some items will not be increased at all while entirely new ones will appear on the stage. (At this point the reader is invited to ask himself whether this result could ever have been reached had we

.treated capital as homogeneous; and to judge the fruitfulness of our method by his answer.)

The capital structure will thus change since the capital coefficients change, almost certainly towards a higher degree of *complexity*, i.e. more types of capital items will now be included in the combinations. The new items, which either did not exist or were not used before, will mostly be of an indivisible character. *Complementarity plus indivisibility* are the essence of the matter. It will not pay to install an indivisible capital good unless there are enough complementary capital goods to justify it. Until the quantity of goods in transit has reached a certain size it does not pay to build a railway. A poor society therefore often uses costlier (at the margin) means of transport than a wealthy one. The accumulation of capital does not merely provide us with the means to build power stations, it also provides us with enough factories to make them pay and enough coal to make them work. Economic progress thus requires a continuously changing composition of the social capital. The new indivisibilities account for the increasing returns.

We must note that the introduction of new indivisible resources, feasible only when the volume of complementary capital reaches a certain size, will as a rule also entail a change in the composition of this complementary capital, with the result that some of these capital goods will have to be shifted to other uses while others, which cannot be shifted, may lose their capital character altogether. Thus the accumulation of capital always destroys some capital, a fundamental fact which economists too often have either ignored or misinterpreted. Such misinterpretation usually takes the form of confining attention to the effects of capital accumulation on income from some capital, and is one of the more sinister results of the homogeneity assumption.

In the light of our argument it is quite wrong to say, for instance, that continuous investment will lower the marginal efficiency of capital. What continuous investment will do is to destroy the capital character of some resources for which the new capital is a substitute, while increasing the incomes from labour and capital resources complementary to it. In conditions of capital change the 'marginal efficiency of capital' (though not Professor Lerner's 'marginal efficiency of investment'!) is thus seen to be a meaningless notion implying, contrary to common observation, that the earning capacity of all capital resources will be affected in the same way.[6]   For similar reasons it is unlikely that 'capital saving' inventions will save much capital, unless the latter happens to be unusually non-specific.

All this has now to be related to Boehm-Bawerk and his third ground.

As Boehm-Bawerk pointed out again and again, his thesis about the higher productivity of roundabout processes is an empirical generalization; it is not derived from the axioms of economic action.   The same applies to our thesis about the typical changes of the capital structure as capital accumulates. There is no *a priori* reason to expect that a sufficient number of exploitable indivisibilities will always present itself, but the history of industrial countries over the last 200 years goes to show that they usually do.   We contend that the circumstances in which Boehm-Bawerk's generalization holds are in general identical with those in which ours holds.

In his replies to critics, notably in his famous *Exkurse*, Boehm-Bawerk reiterated that, in the first place, he did not hold that all lengthening of production processes would cause higher productivity, but only that those 'wisely chosen' would, and that historical experience had convinced him that 'by and large' ('im grossen und ganzen'), as he put it in the first edition of his *Positive Theory of Capital*, or 'as a rule' ('in aller Regel'), as he says in later editions, the lengthening of productive processes would have this result 'with the practical effect that he who wishes and is able to lengthen his productive processes need never be at a loss as to how to improve them'.[7] Boehm-Bawerk also made it clear that his thesis did not mean

[6] This fact has obvious implications for the distribution of incomes.   In a dynamic world it is not possible to say that the accumulation of capital will cause the 'share of capital' to fall relatively to the 'shares' of other factors of production.   In such circumstances the 'share of capital' also becomes a meaningless notion.   What really happens is that some capital owners lose income while others gain.   In a 'capitalistic' economy there are thus always capital owners, but, like the inhabitants of a hotel, they are never for long the same people.   In a world of unexpected change economic forces generate a redistribution of wealth far more pervasive and ineluctable than anything welfare economists could conceive!

[7] *Exkurs I*, 4th ed., p. 3.   Our translation.

that capital could not be increased in any other way than by 'lengthening', but only that, where this is possible, we would soon encounter diminishing returns.[8]

Boehm-Bawerk's thesis thus clearly applies to those cases in which it is possible to invest capital, yet to escape diminishing returns. Which are those cases? Where existing capital is merely duplicated ('widened'), operated by a given labour force, diminishing returns will soon appear. Where new capital resources, but of the type employed before, are being substituted for existing labour ('deepened'), we may have to wait a little longer for diminishing returns to make their appearance, depending on the elasticity of substitution, but appear they will in the end. The only way in which we can hope to resist the pressure of diminishing returns is by changing the composition of capital and enlisting an indivisibility which, with fewer complementary capital resources, could not have been used. 'Higher roundabout productivity' therefore has to be interpreted in terms of this case. The only circumstances which permit it are those circumstances which permit a higher degree of division of capital.

The strong resemblance of our argument to Boehm-Bawerk's can be shown in another way. In Chapter V of Book II of the *Positive Theory*, Boehm-Bawerk introduces the concept of 'stages of maturity' and shows that capital growth will take the form of an increase in the number of these stages. The richer a society the smaller will be the proportion of capital resources used in the 'later stages of production', the stages nearest to the consumption end, and *vice versa*. There can be little doubt that the introduction of these stages, illustrated by the 'concentric rings', constitutes a crucial step in Boehm-Bawerk's argument. We shall attempt to show that these stages find a ready place in our argument.

In an industrial society raw materials have to pass a number of processing stages before they reach the consumer. The accumulation of capital will partly show itself in an increase in this raw material flow, but partly take the form of an increase in the number of processing stages. To the extent to which the latter is the case, a higher degree of the division of capital, as it accompanies the accumulation of capital, will

8 See the discussion with Taussig, *Exkurs I*, pp. 13 ss.

thus be reflected in an increasing specialization of the processing function, in 'vertical disintegration' of the capital structure.[9, 10]   As we see it, these stages are essentially layers of
specialized capital equipment through which the 'original
factors', i.e. raw materials, gradually filter on their journey to
the consuming end.   Progress through capital accumulation
therefore means, firstly, an increase in the number of processing
stages and, secondly, a·change in the composition of the raw
material flow as well as of the capital combinations at each
stage, reflecting specialization as new stages are being added
to the existing structure.

There are, however, two important differences between
Boehm-Bawerk's conception of economic progress and ours.
In the first place, for him all capital is circulating capital,
while for us the layers of specialized capital equipment and
their mode of change are the essence of the matter.   His main
attention was directed to the flow of goods, the 'original
factors' assuming a succession of economic functions as they
change their physical shape on their journey towards the
consumer, while we are more interested in the number and
character of the stages than in the flow that passes them.
Hence, criticism of the whole conception of 'original factors',
as advanced by Professor Knight, does not affect our thesis
as it does Boehm-Bawerk's.   By substituting 'raw materials'
for 'original factors' we may hope to escape Professor Knight's
strictures.

Secondly, and much more important, Boehm-Bawerk, in
trying to find a measure for his flow of goods, found the measure
in time.   His 'stages of maturity' are measured by years of
distance from the consumption end of the process.   In this
way he was led to neglect other important changes which
accompany the accumulation of capital, and exposed himself
to the familiar criticisms.   We, on the other hand, having

[9] This, of course, may take place within the same factory.   The reader will
not fail to notice that we are using the word here in a sense different from that
employed in discussions of economic organization.   All that matters to us is
that the flow of materials successively comes into contact with, and is being
processed by, an increasing number of distinct types of equipment.

[10] In the real world, to be sure, we often find vertical integration of stages of
production.   As a rule this is either a manifestation of oligopoly or of technical
progress, or of both.   As they lie outside the framework of Boehm-Bawerk's
model we need not consider them here.

thus far contrived to tell the story of roundaboutness without mentioning time, must now beware of identifying the whole process with the mere multiplication of processing stages, since we have shown that the capital composition of the intermediate stages changes with each increase in their number. It is only if we make very restrictive assumptions that capital change can be regarded as a function of time.

It seems to us that Boehm-Bawerk, in making time the measure of capital, was led to confuse a process with the dimension in which, *in very special circumstances*, it may take place. Time by itself is not productive, nor is human action necessarily more productive because it takes longer. Boehm-Bawerk was fond of the examples of the growing trees and the ageing wine, but then there are many examples of goods (fruit, flowers) which are spoiled by the lapse of time, a fact he always readily recognized. Yet the third ground is not merely an illegitimate generalization of a segment of experience too narrow to warrant induction. We have seen that the essence of the phenomenon rests in the increasing number of specific processing stages which raw materials, Boehm-Bawerk's 'original factors', have to pass on their way to the consumer. We may imagine these materials spending a certain time at each stage, absorbing the services of the fixed equipment there. Now, if the period spent at each stage *were* given, then an increase in the number of stages would indeed mean an increase in the length of the whole journey. It is only on this assumption that the whole process can be measured in time. If the periods of sojourn at each stage vary as new stages are added, the process as a whole can no longer be measured in time. Time is the dimension of processing only as long as a definite, invariant, time period can be allotted to each processing stage. As we saw, the capital combinations at each stage are bound to vary with the addition of new stages. Hence, the periods of sojourn at each stage cannot remain unchanged as new stages are being added, quite apart from the changing composition of the raw material flow.

We conclude that the accumulation of capital renders possible a higher degree of the division of capital; that capital specialization as a rule takes the form of an increasing number of processing stages and a change in the composition of the raw material flow as well as of the capital combinations at each stage; that the changing pattern of this composition permits the use of new indivisible resources; that these indivisibilities account for increasing returns to capital; and that these increasing returns to the use of capital *are*, in essence, the 'higher productivity of roundabout methods of production'.

These results suggest another, less optimistic, conclusion. If the economic system, as it progresses, evolves an ever more complex pattern of capital complementarity, it is bound to become more vulnerable as it becomes more productive. A household with six servants each of whom is a specialist and none of whom can be substituted for another, is more exposed to individual whims and the vagaries of sickness than one that depends on two or more 'general maids'. Thus an 'expanding economy' is likely to encounter problems of increasing complexity, quite undreamt of in the Harrodian philosophy. For progress to be 'stable' the outputs of the various capital goods would have to be increased in proportion to the changing complementarity pattern, an unlikely feat even in a well-co-ordinated market economy. What this means for the trade cycle we shall see in Chapter VII. Meanwhile the reader may take note that disproportionalities and the resulting maladjustment of the capital structure may give rise to serious problems in economic progress.

CHAPTER VI

CAPITAL STRUCTURE
AND ASSET STRUCTURE

At an early stage of our enquiry we saw that treating capital resources as heterogeneous raises a problem of order; that where the number of relationships between the heterogeneous elements is large and their nature intricate, such order takes the form of a structure; and that in the world of planned human action such structural order ultimately rests on the complementarity of the means employed in a given area of action for distinct ends. We have found two forms of capital complementarity economically significant: the complementarity of the production plan as the direct result of entrepreneurial planning, and the complementarity of the structure of the economic system as a whole, based on the division of labour and capital, as the indirect result of the play of the market forces. We now have to ask whether other forms of capital complementarity exist and, if so, are economically significant.

Thus far, in studying capital complementarity, we have confined our attention mainly to capital goods in the sense of the instruments and materials of physical production. But in Chapter IV we have already learnt that the importance of capital goods lies not in their physical qualities but in the service streams to which they give rise. At the end of that chapter we came to see in the Stock Exchange, which is a market not for physical capital goods but for titles to them, an instrument for promoting consistent capital change.

We now have to take a further step in this direction. We have to ask whether capital complementarity exists outside the sphere of physical capital goods, and, if so, how such forms of capital complementarity are related to those with which we are already familiar. Is there, for instance, economically significant complementarity in a well-selected investment portfolio? If so, by what principles is this complementarity governed? Is there such a thing as an *asset structure* of which the forms of capital structure we have thus far studied are perhaps only particular instances?

In whatever field of action we find human conduct following a recognizable and intelligible order, we shall of course expect to find structural relationships. Without them there could be no theoretical social sciences. Men's buying and selling of assets evidently follows such an order. The markets for assets do not offer a picture of chaos, they are governed by the familiar laws of the market. We therefore need not doubt that an *asset structure* does exist. How it is related to the structure of physical capital hitherto studied is the main question to which this chapter is devoted.

Within the general context of the asset structure the role of money calls for special attention. It will be remembered that in Chapter III we found that, while there can be no production plan without it, we must not treat money as one of our fixed coefficients of production. Variations in the cash balance are our primary criterion of success or failure of the plan. In a world sufficiently dynamic to permit of unexpected change there must be at least one variable to register failure and success. But this fact still does not answer the question what precisely is the difference between money and other capital goods. Moreover, we now have to go farther and ask what is the relationship between money and other assets.

Money is an asset, but it is not a capital good like other elements of a production plan. That it is not, becomes clear as soon as we ask ourselves why and when it is required for carrying out a production project. A cash balance is necessary to buy labour, and current services of capital goods not physically controlled by the planners (water, electric power) during the plan period.[1] But if, as we have to, we regard

---

[1] The fundamental difference between labour and capital as 'factors of production' is of course that in a free society only the services of labour can be hired while as regards capital we usually have a choice of hiring services or buying their source, either outright or embodied in titles to control. The chief justification for a theory of capital of the type here presented lies in the fact that in the buying and selling of capital resources there arise certain economic problems, like capital gains and losses. In a world in which all material resources were inalienable, for instance entailed on the state, but where their services could be freely hired, there would be no more scope for such a theory of capital than there is today for a theory of labour. Problems of capital use and maintenance would of course continue to exist, but offer little scope for a theory on the scale required for a market economy.

these services themselves as 'factor services', i.e. as elements of the plan, we cannot at the same time treat the money that pays for them as a capital good: we should be guilty of double counting. Money is largely, so to speak, a capital good 'by proxy'. It symbolizes, at the initiation of the plan, those current services we shall need later on but which, owing to their 'current' character, we cannot store until we need them. We store the money instead.

The relationship between money and other assets has been a prominent feature of recent attempts to generalize the theory of money, and to expand it into a general theory of assets.[2] Economists who were trying to find a criterion of order for the classification of asset holdings of different composition, devised the notion of a 'liquidity scale' with money as the most liquid asset at one end and completely unsaleable assets at the other. All such endeavours, however, are marred from the outset by the dilemma of having to define 'liquidity' either in terms of money, thus ending up in tautology, or as merely a special case of general commodity preference. In the latter case money is made to lose its specific 'asset' character and function, i.e. to keep the firm out of the bankruptcy court, and is virtually reduced to the rank of ordinary goods. Such are the pleasures of generalization for those who do not stop to reflect upon the intrinsic differences of the objects of their manipulations.

There is a very good reason why we should continue to distinguish between money and other assets on the one hand, and consumer goods and services on the other: In the case of the latter our system of preferences is the ultimate datum behind which we cannot go, while in the case of assets relative preferences are the *explicandum*. Why gramophone records with the music of Irving Berlin find a readier sale than those with the music of Schoenberg is a question about which the economist has nothing to say, but why in an inflation people come to prefer the most illiquid assets to money is a question he can hardly shirk. 'Asset preference' is not an ultimate deter-

[2] Cf. H. Makower and J. Marschak: 'Assets, Prices and Monetary Theory', *Economica*, August 1938, and K. E. Boulding: 'A Liquidity Preference Theory of Market Prices', *Economica*, May 1944.

minant in the sense in which a taste for tobacco is.   We have to ask why at certain times certain people prefer one kind of asset to another.   It follows that a theory of assets cannot be framed on the static model of the General Theory of Consumption.   The composition of asset holdings and its changes make sense only as a response to change, expected and unexpected.

By the same token the distribution of money holdings cannot adequately be explained by 'liquidity preference'.   Monetary change, as we saw in Chapter III, is sometimes the concomitant, and sometimes the ulterior consequence of other asset changes, unexpected and, as often as not, undesired.   An explanation of such changes as 'exchange governed by preference' entirely misses the point.   Not a theory of assets based on immutable (at least by endogenous forces) preference, but a Theory of Business Finance based on our knowledge of entrepreneurial action in response to change, expected and unexpected, is what we need.   To set out at least the elements of such a theory, couched in terms of plan and process, is the main task of this chapter.

We shall start by classifying assets.   Since, however, our purpose is praxeological, not merely taxonomic, since our interest is in assets *qua* instruments of action and the structural relationships between them as channels for the transmission of knowledge, our mode of classification is governed by the relevance of our classes to planning and action.

In the first place we distinguish between *operating assets* and *securities*, i.e. between physical capital goods and money complementary to them on the one hand, and the titles which embody the control of production as well as define the recipients of payments, on the other hand.   At each moment, superficially, the complementarity pattern of the former is governed by the exigencies of production planning, the structure of the latter by the 'asset preference' of the holders of titles.   But in the same way as the technical exigencies of production planning reflect past experience and its interpretation in the form of expectations presently held, and are continuously changing as the latter are tested and present becomes past, asset preferences change and holdings are reshuffled as experience and new knowledge direct.   To understand how the two spheres of action interact is to understand how a market economy works.

Among the operating assets we have next to distinguish between *first-line assets*, *second-line assets*, and *reserve assets*. By first-line assets we mean those capital goods (machines, conveyor belts, lifts) whose services provide the input of the production plan right from the start. Second-line assets are those operating assets which, like spare parts, or money for wage payments, are planned to be put into operation at a definite point of time during the plan period. They will either be required physically or, as in the case of money, are capital assets only 'by proxy' and will later on be replaced by 'real services' of labour or other capital goods whose services will be hired. Reserve assets are those, like the cash reserve or reserve stocks, of which it is hoped that if all goes well they will not have to be thrown in at all. Reserve assets are therefore held against unforeseen contingencies, they are not meant to be brought into operation at a definite time. They are operating assets to which, in contrast to the others, no definite period of operation has been assigned in the plan. As we said above (p. 42), reserve assets are *supplementary*, not *complementary* to the first- and second-line assets. Whether they ever will become complementary to them depends on chance.

In an uncertain world the universal need for reserve assets sets a limit to the fixity of the coefficients of production. We are now able to understand why unexpected changes in the magnitude of the reserve assets provide a criterion for success or failure of the plan: Success means that the reserves did not have to be thrown in, extreme failure means the complete exhaustion of the reserves.

If the plan turns out to be successful, it may be possible in the next period to absorb some of the reserve assets in an expansion of the original plan without increasing the risk. While a fall in reserve assets without an increase in other assets means that reserves thrown in have to replace casualties, and cannot serve to exploit success.

Next we have to classify securities. For our purpose we need go no further than drawing the general distinction between *debt-titles* embodying the right to an income in terms of currency units, and *equities* embodying the right to participate in control and in residual income. We shall see that the various modes the relationship between debt and equity may assume, the 'high' or 'low gear' of the company's capital, or, as we shall call it, its *control structure*, is of considerable importance in determining the response to success and failure.

We are here dealing with a phenomenon which has been much affected by recent historical changes the impact of which is not always well understood. In the old family firm ownership and control were in the same hands, while unlimited liability confined the possibility of incurring debt to narrow proportions by making it very risky to both creditor and debtor. But it is wrong to think that in the modern company the link between equity ownership and control is entirely broken. The relationship, no longer one of identity, has merely been modified. Those who speak of complete 'separation of ownership and control' forget the impact of failure and crisis. They evidently think of conditions in which all plans succeed and expansion is easily financed by 'ploughing back' profits. But this need not be so. In a world of unexpected change a long and unbroken record of success is likely to be rare, and for our purposes the study of such cases is not likely to be very profitable. A theory of capital relationships based on the assumption of invariable success of plans is apt to lead to wrong conclusions when applied to a world of unexpected change.

It would seem, then, that there are three kinds of structure: The *Plan Structure* based on technical complementarity, the *Control Structure* based on high or low gear of the company's capital, and the *Portfolio Structure* based on people's asset preference. These three structures are not independent of each other. Whether a given production plan with its accoutrement of plant, equipment, raw materials, etc., is at all feasible depends *inter alia* on whether people are willing to take up the securities necessary to finance it, and this in its turn will depend on whether debentures, preference shares, or common stock are offered to them, and in what proportions.

Nor, as we pointed out already, can 'asset preference' be regarded as being independent of expectations regarding managerial competence and conduct in making and carrying out plans. In this, too, it is very different from consumers' preference, since a cigarette smoker in his choice is confined to what is available in the shops with no need to ponder the managerial efficiency of the makers of the various brands.

The scene is now set for our study of the dynamic relationships between the various classes of assets and the structures they form. We shall study the forces which 'integrate' our three structures into an over-all *asset structure*, i.e. the forces bringing the decisions which shape them into consistency with each other. This they do, and can only do, by transmitting knowledge. It is of some importance that the actions they prompt will either take the form of money payments, or at least foreshadow or create the conditions for such payments.

Thus a new enterprise is started by somebody putting up money. At first all operating assets are money assets. Gradually, as the plan comes into operation, most of the money is exchanged for capital goods and 'real services' which become input, and so the plan structure begins to take shape. Conversely, when the enterprise is liquidated, all first- and second-line assets are turned into money which is then distributed to the holders of securities in the order of their claims. Between these two points of time we have to distinguish, first of all, between what happens in conditions of expected success, 'success according to plan', and in conditions of unexpected change.

As long as success is achieved 'according to plan' the structural relationships remain undisturbed. Reserve assets neither increase nor decrease, operating cash balances and stocks are being replenished out of gross revenue. A steady yield stream in the form of money payments flows from cash balances to the holders of securities who, getting what they expected to get, will probably see little reason for changing the composition of their portfolios. The picture is that of stationary conditions with a 'steady income stream' flowing year after year, giving no incentive to anybody to modify his conduct.

If success is unexpectedly great problems begin to arise. The surplus profits ('surplus', of course, in the sense of: unexpected) have to be assigned to somebody. They may be used for higher dividends or be 'ploughed back' or serve to pay off debts.[3]   In the first case they will, in addition to giving higher incomes, entail capital gains to shareholders, and hence change the total value as well as the composition of their portfolios.   In the second case they will induce and make possible a new plan structure.   In the third case they will modify the control structure.   The decision will be made by the equity holders, but it is a well-known fact that the managers are as a rule able to influence their decision by withholding knowledge from them, by 'hiding' part of the surplus profits, in order to keep them under their own supervision.[4]

We now come to the case of failure.   Temporary failure need mean nothing worse than a temporary drain on the reserves.   If there were ample reserves to start with, a reduction of cash reserves may suffice to enable the firm to weather the storm.   But where the money cushion is inadequate, or the failure severe, other steps will have to be taken.   The balance of operating assets may be upset.   It may become impossible to replace such assets as they wear out.   Sooner or later the need for a reshuffle of operating assets will present itself.   Such a reshuffle will almost certainly involve a need for more money, partly because, as we saw in Chapter III, the proceeds from the sale of old capital goods may not cover the cost of the new, and partly because the cash balance has to be replenished.   Thus both expansion following on success as well as reconstruction following failure cause the 'demand for money' to increase.   But the conditions in which it is demanded, and the terms on which it is supplied, will differ in both cases.   A successful enterprise will not ordinarily experience great difficulty in finding new money capital for expansion,

[3] A degree of risk does not attach to a given investment project as such, but always depends on the control structure.   There are many projects which a young and heavily indebted firm would not dare to touch, but which an old firm with low debt and ample reserves can afford to take in its stride.   In this fact lies an important obstacle, often overlooked, to effective competition, at least in the short run.

[4] This is not to deny that in practice there is often something to be said for stabilizing the rate of dividend and 'ploughing back' profits in good years.   All we wish to say is that in general the successful functioning of a market economy requires the widest possible diffusion of knowledge   It is of course always possible that people will draw wrong conclusions from facts correctly stated, but this is no reason for withholding information from them.   The justification offered for hiding profits is often that shareholders, if they knew the true profits, would make irresponsible claims and thus jeopardize future earnings.   This may be so, but the other half of the argument rests on an assumption of managerial infallibility and omniscience not often borne out by the facts.

though the new capital may alter the control structure. With
a record of success behind them the managers of successful
companies as a rule are not easily discouraged by fear of
losing control. In a successful company, moreover, this
danger can in any case usually be averted by an issue of 'rights'
to existing shareholders at par or above, but below the market
price of the shares.

But financial reconstruction of an unsuccessful enterprise is a
different matter, as the mere fact of the need for it transmits
knowledge about the past performance of the management.
Hence such reconstruction is usually postponed as long as is
possible.[5] A change in the control structure is now indicated.
Whether or not the existing common stock is actually 'written
down', its value will have declined, not as a result of any
decline in 'asset preference', but as the result of events outside
the control of the asset holders. It may be that debenture
holders and other creditors have to take over the enterprise
and to appoint a new management. Or, ultimately, they
may even have to liquidate it.

Capital gains and losses accompany the success and failure of
production plans. They are of great importance in a market
economy, though modern economics with its emphasis on
output and incomes has for too long tended to ignore them.
Yet it is obvious that consumption will be strongly stimulated
by capital gains and discouraged by losses. Moreover, as we
just saw, capital losses may give rise to a demand for capital
to finance reconstruction.

For our purpose in this chapter capital gains and losses are
of importance mainly in that they reflect within the portfolio
structure the success or failure of production plans, and thus
record within one sphere the events that have taken place, or
are about to take place, within another sphere. Their integrating quality is inherent in this function. Capital gains and
losses modify the portfolio structure by affecting the relative
values of the components of investment portfolios. If we wish
to say that this structure is determined by relative preference
for different classes of assets, we must nevertheless remember

---

[5] A reconstruction of a company often takes place when the directors know
already that the situation is improving, but preference shareholders and creditors
do not. The directors therefore are prepared to offer terms to them that the
creditors do not know enough to refuse.

that such preferences are not given to us as a 'datum', but merely reflect other economic processes and their interpretation by asset holders.

Capital gains and losses are not the direct result of money flows, though, as in the case of higher dividends, they may be an indirect result. Essentially they reflect in one sphere events, or the expectation of events, the occurrence of which in another sphere is indicated, and knowledge of which is transmitted, by changes in money flows.

Whether or not such capital gains and losses are accompanied by changes in the financial circulation is for us irrelevant. Whether or not a price change in a market is accompanied by much or little trading depends on the diffusion of expectations, on whether the whole market interprets an event in the same way, or whether there are marked differences of interpretation.

From this rather fragmentary survey of interrelationships in the capital sphere we conclude:

Firstly, that changes in the size of reserve assets, and particularly of the cash reserve, serve as primary criteria of success and failure. Money flows, on the other hand, by regulating the size of cash balances, integrate the over-all asset structure and make for consistent capital change. As long as money flows regularly from cash balances to title holders in such a way as to leave cash balances undepleted, it indicates planned success. Where the flow increases, it drains off excess cash and records unplanned success. When the flow ceases altogether, it records failure. When it is actually reversed, when money flows from title holders into cash balances, it corrects the size of the latter by replenishing them.

Secondly, processes involving transmission of knowledge bring the various constituents of the asset structure into consistency with each other, modifying the control structure and the composition of portfolios. In these processes revaluation of securities by the market plays a vital part. Capital gains and losses are changes in asset values reflecting changes in other elements of the asset structure. It is therefore, thirdly, impossible to treat the demand for securities as though it were a demand for consumption goods. In the theory of consumption we assume that all the consumer has to do is to

bring a number of 'urges', external data to him as to us, into
a logical and coherent order.   This is a problem in the Pure
Logic of Choice.   But the asset holder has to *interpret* and *apply*
the facts he learns about in the light of his knowledge.   This
is not a matter of pure logic.

Fourth, failure means loss of assets and the need to create
new assets, short of complete liquidation of the enterprise.
The creation of new assets means new investment opportunities.   Even where the new assets are money assets this is so,
for the money needed for cash balances to sustain production
processes is 'money for use', not 'idle money'.   Its accumulation is merely the first step in a process of purchasing services.
And to the extent to which failure has led to a loss of assets
other than monetary, for instance, by under-maintenance of
fixed capital or non-replacement of stocks, the investment
opportunity opened up by the need for replacement is obvious.
But if failure is not simply to be repeated, and except in the
special case where failure is merely due to bad timing, replenish-
ment of cash has to be accompanied by a reshuffle of other
capital goods.   This fact, as we shall see in Chapter VII, has
some important consequences for 'cheap money' and similar
policies.   In a depression, to be sure, 'cheap money' has its
part to play, but in conjunction with other forms of business
reconstruction, not as a substitute for them!

We have so far assumed a simple type of asset structure in
which all securities directly 'represent' operating assets.   This
of course need not be so.   There are securities 'representing'
other securities which on their part 'represent' further securities.
Nor need these securities all belong to the same type: The
equity of one company may consist of a loan to another, while
the debentures issued by a third company may serve the
purpose of financing the equity of a fourth.   Such 'securities
pyramids' may appear in various forms and serve various ends.
Investment trusts are usually formed for the diversification of
risk, while holding companies as often as not serve the purpose
of centralization of control.   What is of interest to us is that
where control over a number of subsidiaries is vested in a
holding company, the case is exactly parallel to that of entrepreneurial control over the operating assets in the 'unit firm': In
both cases the unity of control engenders a unity of plan, so

that we have here a case of plan complementarity.   It follows that in the same way as plan revision will often lead to a regrouping of operating assets in the simple case we considered in Chapter III, in the more complex cases the reshuffle of assets will take the form of a reshuffle of subsidiary companies forming part of the 'General Plan' control over which is vested in the holding company.   In fact, in the modern world of large-scale enterprise the typical objects of reshuffling are as often as not whole subsidiary companies.   The type of analysis presented in Chapter III is fully applicable to such cases.

This fact, as we shall see in the next chapter, is of some significance in business fluctuations.   The regrouping of assets made necessary by a 'crisis', i.e. plan failure in large sectors of the economy, cannot as a rule be confined to reshuffling of first-line assets and replenishing cash balances.   Whole concerns and, perhaps, industries may have to be regrouped and reorganized.   The challenge of widespread failure to true entrepreneurship can rarely be met by making minor adjustments.

All this has some bearing on the question of the location of entrepreneurial control in modern joint-stock enterprise. We hear it often said that in the modern industrial world the managers who make decisions about investment, production, and sales *are* 'the entrepreneurs', while capital owners have been reduced to a merely passive role.   The 'separation of ownership and control' is the phrase used to describe this state of affairs.   In fact the shareholder is already widely regarded as a mere rentier, dependent for his living on the exertions of the allegedly more active members of the enterprise, and unable to influence events.   The calm and unruffled atmosphere in which most company meetings take place is offered as evidence for this thesis.   If it were true it would of course obviate our concept of the control structure.   If equity ownership has nothing to do with control and the making of decisions, the whole structural scheme we have presented would fall to the ground.

But the argument appears to be based on a fundamental praxeological misconception.   No doubt, he who decides on action is 'active'; but so is he who creates the conditions in which the decision-maker acts. We have endeavoured to explain that the asset structure of the enterprise is a complex network of relationships, transmitting knowledge and the incentive to action from one group to another. The notion of the capital owner as a merely passive recipient of residual income is clearly incompatible with that view.

In point of fact the manager and the capital owner are each active in his own distinct sphere, but their spheres of action are interrelated by virtue of mutual orientation. For either the other's action is a datum of his own action. The manager's plans concern operating assets. He operates and regroups them as his plans succeed or fail. The availability of new capital for expansion in case of success or reconstruction in case of failure is for him a datum. The capital owner's plans concern securities. He has to regroup them in the same way as the manager regroups his operating assets, and managerial decisions determine the scope of his operations as his decisions determine that of the manager. It is true that the modern shareholder rarely takes the trouble of opposing managerial decisions with which he happens to disagree at the company meeting. But this is so because he has a more effective way of voting against these decisions: He sells.

Our main argument in this chapter has been based on a simple division of assets into operating assets and securities. But we saw in the case of the holding company controlling a number of subsidiaries that it is sometimes impossible to draw such a clear dividing line. In such cases it often becomes impossible to say when, for instance, a certain sale or purchase of securities involves a 'managerial decision' and when it does not. In the same way it becomes impossible to disentangle profits and capital gains. If by entrepreneurial decisions we mean decisions involving the making and revising of plans, there is no difference between changing a production plan and changing the composition of an investment portfolio. They are both exactly the same type of action.

For the sake of terminological clarity it is desirable to call an 'entrepreneur' anybody who is concerned with the management of assets.[6] At the end of Chapter I we pointed out

[6] See F. A. Hayek: *Profits, Interest and Investment*, 1939, pp. 119–20.

that, as regards capital, the function of the entrepreneur consists in specifying and modifying the concrete form of the capital resources committed to his care.

We might then distinguish between the capitalist-entrepreneur and the manager-entrepreneur. The only significant difference between the two lies in that the specifying and modifying decisions of the manager presuppose and are consequent upon the decisions of the capitalist. If we like, we may say that the latter's decisions are of a 'higher order'.

Thus a capitalist makes a first specifying decision by deciding to invest a certain amount of capital, which probably, though not necessarily, exists in the money form, in Company A rather than in Company B, or rather than to lend it to the government. The managers of Company A then make a second specifying decision by deciding to use the capital so received in building or extending a department store in one suburb rather than another suburb, or another city. The manager of this local department store makes further specifying decisions, and so on, until the capital has been converted into concrete assets.

All these decisions are specifying decisions. In principle, there is no difference between them, and there seems little point in drawing dividing lines between those who make them. It is only when we realize what the heterogeneity of capital means that we come to understand what an entrepreneur is and does.

CHAPTER VII

CAPITAL IN THE TRADE CYCLE

In what follows we shall make use of our newly acquired knowledge of structural relationships between assets in general, and capital goods in particular, in order to elucidate some problems of the Trade Cycle. By 'Trade Cycle' we shall mean nothing more precise than the periodic ups and downs of output, incomes, and employment to which modern industrial economies seem to be prone. We do not assume a high degree of uniformity between successive fluctuations, but just enough similarity to make comparison possible. As Professor Hicks has said, 'We ought not to expect that actual cycles will repeat each other at all closely. Certainly the cycles of reality do not repeat each other; they have, at the most, a family likeness.'[1]

The task of trade cycle theory is therefore not confined, as it has been so often in the past, to explaining the similarities of successive fluctuations. The dissimilarities also have to be accounted for. It is certainly our task to indicate causes for downturn and upturn, and to analyse the cumulative processes of expansion and contraction. But on the evidence we have no right to believe that these causes will always be the same, nor to doubt that their relative force will vary from case to case. Similar causes will of course produce similar results. The dissimilarites we observe have then to be explained by the large number of potential causes not all of which become actual in each instance. The similarities are too many for the group of possible causes to be very large, but the dissimilarities are too many for it to be very small.

The Trade Cycle cannot be appropriately described by means of one theoretical model. We need a number of models each showing what happens when certain potential causes become operative. The many models that have been constructed by economists in the past are therefore not necessarily incompatible with each other. Overinvestment and

[1] J. R. Hicks: *A Contribution to the Theory of the Trade Cycle*, 1950, p. 108.

underconsumption theories, for instance, are not mutually exclusive. None of them of course is the true theory of the Trade Cycle; each is probably an unduly broad generalization of certain historical facts. Once we admit the dissimilarity of different historical fluctuations we can no longer look for an identical explanation. In dealing with industrial and financial fluctuations eclecticism is the proper attitude to take. There is little reason to believe that the causes of the crisis of 1929 were the same as those of the crisis of 1873.

Of late this has come to be more widely recognized. Professor Hicks, for instance, distinguishes between 'weak booms' which 'die by working themselves out' and which lend themselves to an underconsumptionist explanation, and 'strong booms' which end by 'hitting the ceiling' and in the explanation of which scarcity of productive services must play a part. And a feeling of the immense complexity of trade cycle problems is fairly noticeable in many quarters.

There can of course be no question of our traversing the whole immense field in this chapter, nor even of our reviewing the literature of the past twenty years. Our aim is to elucidate some trade cycle problems, it is not to set forth a new trade cycle theory. The day of 'comprehensive' trade cycles theories is long past. For our part, our interest in the matter is largely, though not exclusively, confined to the exploration of the part played by *structural maladjustment*. We see no reason to believe that its influence is ubiquitous, but even less to doubt that in many cases it is pronounced. In this connection the 'strong boom' is of particular interest to us. Where the capital resources available for investment prove to be inadequate, their composition cannot be a matter of indifference. We have here evidently an instance of *inconsistent capital change*.

The Hicksian theory of the trade cycle is a theory of the strong boom. We shall therefore in this chapter start with a critical examination of certain of its features. In doing so we shall encounter certain difficulties which arise from the assumption, implicit in most of Professor Hicks' theory, that all capital is homogeneous. We shall then find that some of these difficulties can be met by introducing assumptions about the capital structure and its distortion in a strong boom which

H

appear to follow from the main argument of this book.   Finally
we shall survey the situation on the morrow of the downturn
and study the measures necessary for readjustment, in particular the forms of capital regrouping which, if undertaken
in time, would prevent a further deterioration of the situation.

I

In the Hicksian model investment plays the most prominent
part in generating the cycle.   Investment means the creation
of new capital goods.   Yet Professor Hicks, while he has
much to say about investment, has little to say about capital.
A theory of investment without a theory of capital, however,
is very much like Hamlet without the Prince.   Now, Professor
Hicks regards the cyclical vicissitudes he describes as a concomitant of an 'expanding economy'.   It might be held
that in dealing with economic expansion we are only interested
in rates of expansion, and not in the expanding magnitudes
themselves.   In fact, the whole purpose of Professor Hicks'
model is to show how unequal rates of expansion engender
cyclical fluctuations.   But if the cause of the unequal rates of
expansion lies in the expanding magnitudes themselves, the
latter cannot simply be ignored.   Where these magnitudes
change their composition in the process, a theoretical model
which neglects such change must be regarded as inadequate.
Ultimately, this consequence of the heterogeneity of resources
must produce 'structural stress' and thus cause the rate of
capital expansion to slow down.   The neglect of this fact in
the Hicksian model leads to certain difficulties.   Of these we
shall give three examples.

First, Professor Hicks, following Mr. Harrod, makes much
of the 'background of economic expansion' against which his
model is set; but about the forces engendering this expansion
remarkably little is said.   Several times[2] we are told that
expansion may be due either to growth of population or 'due
to many of the various causes which can be grouped together
as increasing productivity'.[3]   This of course may simply mean

[2] See, for instance, pp. 13n, 36.   [3] Ibid., p. 8.

technical progress. But what about the division of labour and capital as forces of progress, and their implications?

We saw in Chapter V that the division of capital entails a change in the composition of capital in the direction of more complex complementarity, and that such change usually takes the form of increasing prevalence of fixed capital. How is this fact accounted for in the Hicksian model? It would appear to be covered by the 'long-range' investment (p. 59) much of which (but how much?) is included in the notion of *autonomous investment*. Many critics of Professor Hicks' work have pointed out what a vague and unsatisfactory notion Autonomous Investment is, and that instead of being formally defined its meaning is merely illustrated by means of enumeration of a few examples. Be that as it may, for our purposes the distinction between Autonomous and Induced Investment proves particularly unfortunate in that it separates conceptually what economically is inseparable because complementary. Economic progress, where it is not due to changes in technical knowledge, is largely the result of a changing combination of an increasing number of specific capital resources, some of them indivisible. If some of these are the product of autonomous, some of induced investment, as all working capital evidently is, we can gain no clear and comprehensive picture of their *modus cooperandi*.

This is of course due to the fact that Professor Hicks' interest is confined to the relationship between changes in output and quantitative change in (some) capital. Professor Hicks does not discuss the effect of capital change on output, or rather, the latter effect is partly *subsumed* in the general results of autonomous investment, and partly in the magnitude of the Accelerator. The changes in the composition of C without which Y cannot grow are disregarded, and this makes a correct understanding of the vicissitudes which befall the economic system at the 'ceiling' all but impossible. We shall later on return to the subject of autonomous and induced investment. Meanwhile we shall note that the source of the trouble evidently lies in the implicit assumption that all capital is homogeneous.

Secondly, in the Hicksian model the acceleration coefficient 'v' plays a vital part. It is assumed to remain constant throughout the upswing of the cycle, as well as between cycles.

Critics like Professor Lundberg[4] have pointed out that this is a highly unrealistic assumption to make. In shipping 'v' must be higher than in the grocery trade. As $\dfrac{C}{Y}$ varies in different industries, so does $\dfrac{dC}{dY}$. It is readily seen that, again, the difficulty is due to the implied assumption that all capital is homogeneous. In fact, it might almost be said that Professor Hicks has forced the 'constant v' hypothesis upon himself. Of course, even if all capital were homogeneous, the ratio of capital to output might still be different in different industries, and the cause of such variations would still have to be explained. But there can be little doubt that in reality qualitative heterogeneity of capital is the most frequent cause of quantitative variations in the Accelerator, for instance the different ratio of fixed to working capital in different industries. As long as we remain oblivious of this fact we cannot account for these variations and shall tend to disregard them; hence the assumption of a constant accelerator.

Third, when Professor Hicks comes to grapple with the problem of the 'ceiling' he has to drop the homogeneity assumption. It is easy to see why: Were he to follow Keynes in assuming complete homogeneity of all resources, there would be no ceiling at all. There would only be a point of full employment, and beyond it the realm of inflation. Multiplier and accelerator being what they are, there is no more reason why our economic system, once set in motion, should stop at this particular point rather than at any other. Evidently the reason for the existence of the ceiling has to be sought in unequal expansibility in different sectors which cannot be overcome by intersectional transfer of resources. But Professor Hicks employs only two 'sectional ceilings', and hence only one heterogeneity. 'Let us therefore suppose (as is realistic) that different sorts of resources are specialized to the production of investment goods and consumption goods respectively; and consider what happens if the production of investment goods reaches its ceiling at a time when the production of consumption goods is still capable of further expansion.'[5]

[4] E. Lundberg: 'Om Ekonomiska Expansionens Stabilitet', *Ekonomisk Tidskrift*, September 1950.   [5] Ibid., p. 128.

It is true that later on he admits, 'We could easily have made a further advance by splitting up these ceilings, and allowing a sectional ceiling for every product . . . but I do not think that it would make much difference to the argument.'[6] In some ways, however, it can be shown that it would make a difference.

The reality of the ceiling has been doubted by one of Professor Hicks' critics.[7] It is perhaps not surprising that a generation brought up on an intellectual diet of Keynesianism and memories of 1929 should no longer be able to grasp the meaning of a strong boom. There can be little doubt that in history strong booms have 'hit the ceiling', i.e. been checked by a scarcity of resources. But where are we to look for the manifestations of scarcity? We suggest that, historically speaking, they are primarily to be found in the sphere of industrial raw materials, that in the past the *raw material ceiling* has been the sectional ceiling of crucial importance.

In his interesting study of *World Production, Prices and Trade, 1870–1960*[8] Professor W. A. Lewis has computed 'terms of trade' for industrial raw materials (primary products other than food), viz. the ratio of their prices to those of manufactured goods. His statistics show that between 1870 and 1913 all the years in which the index (1913 = 100) reaches or passes the 100 mark were 'boom top years'.

1872	1873	1900	1907 [9]
100·9	101·7	101·1	100·0

These, then, were years in which industrial raw materials became relatively scarce.

The argument gains further support from the cyclical record of the divergence of the index number of the quantity of international trade in primary products, C_T, from that of the world production of manufactures (excluding the U.S.A. and the U.S.S.R.), M_N. Professor Lewis finds that over the period 1881 to 1929 'a 1 per cent increase in world manufacturing is associated with an 0·87 per cent increase in world trade in primary products' (p. 113).

[6] Ibid., p. 132.
[7] J. S. Duesenberry: 'Hicks on the Trade Cycle', *Quarterly Journal of Economics*, May 1950.
[8] *The Manchester School of Economic and Social Studies*, May 1952.
[9] Table II, col. 11, p. 117.

The annual divergencies from this ratio bear an obvious relation to the trade cycle.

'PERCENTAGE DIVERGENCE BETWEEN ACTUAL AND CALCULATED C_T

1882	− 3·9	1890	− 2·1	1900	− 5·4	1907	− 1·0
83	− 3·1	91	0·7	01	0·0	08	− 1·6
84	− 0·6	92	1·6	02	− 0·2	09	3·6
85	− 1·0	93	0·0	03	2·6	10	− 0·8
86	4·4	94	1·9	04	1·7	11	1·3
87	0·7	95	4·0	05	2·5	12	4·2
88	− 2·8	96	0·7	06	2·6	13	1·4
89	− 2·6	97	2·6	07	− 1·0		
1890	− 2·1	98	2·7				
		99	− 0·9				
		1900	− 5·4				

The minuses, it will be seen, appear at the top and bottom of each column, the boom years, while the pluses are in the middle' (p. 114).

Professor Lewis' interpretation of these figures is: 'Stocks of primary products are accumulated by importing countries during the slump, and are used up during the boom.' But this interpretation is both, factually and analytically, open to doubt. By no stretch of the imagination can years like 1895, 1905, and 1912, all years of strong positive deviation, be called slump years. In these years world production of manufactures (excluding Russia) increased by 9·8, 10·6, and 8·7 per cent respectively while their secular trend rate of annual increase was 3·6 per cent (p. 126). In these years, then, the expansion of raw material production not merely kept in step with, but actually exceeded the rate of industrial expansion. There was no raw material ceiling and general expansion continued unhampered.

Moreover, Professor Lewis' interpretation is pre-Hicksian, ignores the ceiling, and is based on underconsumptionist premises. The true explanation appears to be that in 1872–3, 1890, 1900 and 1907 manufacturing industries ran into a raw material ceiling. We conclude that the raw material ceiling has often been of fairly decisive importance.[10]

[10] What is said in the text applies to industrial raw materials only. Food production is a different matter. The 'terms of trade' for food do not appear to follow a cyclical pattern.

Professor Hicks speaks of an investment goods ceiling. Investment goods may be broadly, though not inadequately, divided into industrial raw materials and fixed capital goods. Can we treat the two together in the way Professor Hicks does? Can we assume that the two sub-ceilings are hit at the same point of time? We may doubt it, since if it were so, why do the intersectional terms of trade fluctuate so much? If the two sub-ceilings are not hit at the same time, but the raw material ceiling reached first, there will be fixed capital goods which cannot come into full operation, at least not in the way such operation was planned *ex ante*, owing to lack of their working capital complements. They will provide a peculiar kind of unplanned 'excess capacity' and constitute a phenomenon which appears to be of crucial importance. Unless the various 'investment goods sub-ceilings' are all encountered at the same moment (and why should they?) the emergence of this 'dynamic excess capacity' is almost inevitable.

It might be said that raw material prices being more flexible than fixed capital goods prices, relative price figures tell us little about relative scarcity. It is true that a fixed capital goods ceiling will manifest itself, at least at first, in delayed delivery rather than in higher prices, so that absence of higher prices does not necessarily mean absence of excess demand. But the delay in delivery can only postpone, and not prevent, the emergence of excess capacity, unless of course the raw material shortage is merely temporary, not a *'ceiling'* but a 'bottleneck'. The mere fact that after both sub-ceilings have been reached the output of both, raw materials and fixed capital goods, will slow down, is irrelevant. It is relative scarcity of complementary factors which here causes excess capacity and upsets plans. For no factor can be used in isolation, complementarity is of the essence of all plans, and withdrawal of a factor, or its failure to turn up at the appointed time, will equally endanger the success of the production plans.

We have just dealt with a phenomenon which occurs *before* the new capital combinations can be taken into use. We must now ask what happens afterwards.

The effect of capital investment on output raises a number of questions, not merely of 'effective demand', of consumption keeping in step with output. If we were dealing with a weak boom, these would be the most relevant questions to ask. But the effect of investment on output also depends, and certainly in a strong boom, on the degree of complementarity of the different capital resources employed, in other words on the degree of consistency of such capital change. This raises a number of questions which, to our knowledge, have rarely, if ever, been asked, at least in the field of trade cycle theory.

We said above that the distinction between autonomous and induced investment is, for our purposes, unfortunate since it tends to separate conceptually what economically is inseparable because complementary. But at the same time its critical examination will afford us a welcome opportunity for a study of forms of consistent and inconsistent capital change accompanying industrial fluctuations. By elucidating the nature of those economic forces which make the various forms of capital change inseparable we may hope to learn a good deal about the direct and indirect effects of investment on output.

The relationship between autonomous and induced investment may be viewed from three different angles.

First, the two in general are complementary as they jointly determine total incomes and employment. This is the aspect in which Professor Hicks is chiefly interested.

Secondly, at or near the ceiling they begin to compete for resources. In fact, here a 'dip' in autonomous investment at the right moment would give induced investment a 'breathing space' before the ceiling is hit. This is implicit in the whole argument.

Third, there is the much larger issue which concerns us here: the complementarity of the products of the two types of investment, the actual capital resources, after they have taken shape. Professor Hicks does not deal with this question; if it has any place in his model it is subsumed in the slope of the ceiling.

If any structural complementarity exists between the capital resources in an economic system, this clearly is an important problem. Variations in the rate of the two types of investment must have some effect on the productivity of the capital resources produced. Some of these variations at least must fall into the class of inconsistent capital changes. This is clearly seen in the case of induced investment which depends on the rate of increase of output, hence is not independent of the productivity of earlier investment, both autonomous and induced.

Structural complementarity of course does not mean fixed coefficients of production. We saw above (p. 42) that in an uncertain world the need for reserves sets a limit to the fixity of the coefficients of production within the framework of a plan. What is true for the complementarity of the production plan is equally true for structural complementarity, only that the place of the reserve assets is here taken by various forms of 'excess capacity'. There must be some flexibility in the over-all capital structure. Transport and power resources, for instance, must be such as to permit some growth and re-grouping of secondary industries, and the same applies to all raw material production. It would be wrong to think that consistent capital change in the growth of autonomous and induced capital requires a one-to-one, or any other fixed relationship. On the contrary, a certain excess capacity, for instance in transport and power production, is necessary if a position is to be avoided in which any increase in capital in one industry requires a corresponding decline in another. It is just such excess capacity that makes a large number of capital changes in secondary industries consistent with each other. But all this means is that there is, in an industrial economy, as a rule a fairly wide range over which variations in the different rates of investment would be consistent changes. It does not mean that inconsistent change cannot exist.

There certainly can be too much autonomous investment relatively to induced, so that we have too much autonomous capital and too little induced. Or it may be the other way round: induced investment pushing against the ceiling which is the result of too little autonomous investment in the past, for instance a raw material capacity ceiling as indicated by Professor Lewis' tables. Neither of course could happen in a Keynesian world, a world without ceilings and scarce resources, or at least there it would mean at worst a temporary hitch, a 'bottleneck', until 'the other' kind of investment has caught up. But in an economy moving near the ceiling scarce resources, once committed, may not find complements, however long we may wait. Excessive railway construction may not merely be a waste of present resources, it may also have the

effect of depriving the railways of future traffic by depriving
railway customers of capital.

There can be little doubt, for instance, that the industrial
development of Switzerland between 1850 and 1900 was
gravely hampered by excessive railway building owing to the
fact that the oligopolistic nature of the railway market made
it necessary to stake claims by building lines long ahead of any
possibility of their profitable use. The resulting capital
shortage for a time provided a serious obstacle to the growth
of Swiss industries.[11]

In a strong boom investment plans are started for which
adequate resources do not exist and which must therefore fail.
What is worse, even the available resources are wasted by
being given a form which for its effective use would depend
upon the support of other resources which are not available.
Not only are there too few resources, but the few are 'scattered'
over too wide a field; they lack the support of other resources
which would have rendered them more productive in their
present uses than they are now.

We doubt whether the distinction between autonomous and
induced investment can easily be made in practice; in many
cases it would be most difficult to make it. We used this
Hicksian pair of concepts merely to show that even if the
distinction could be made conceptually as regards the form of
investment, it cannot meaningfully be made as regards the
resultant capital types. The resultant capital resources will
have to be complementary, and if the two capital changes are
inconsistent with each other there will be trouble, viz. inter-
ruption of the continuous investment process, even if the
resource needs of the two types of investment did not clash
at the ceiling. Neither autonomous nor induced investment
is in fact independent of forces which, in their turn, depend
on the degree of mutual consistency of the two types of
investment.

Exception may be taken to the view here set forth on the
ground that we have failed to distinguish between 'economic
growth' and 'cyclical fluctuations', and confused phenomena

---

[11] Of course we do not mean to deny that in the evolution of the economy
of Western Europe the Swiss railways provided an indispensable link. But for
a time the link was bigger than it need have been.

of the 'long run' with those of the 'short run'.[12] But in the light of what we have just said such an exception cannot be sustained.

The distinction between the long and the short run referred originally to the change in resources which occurs in the former, but not in the latter, where such change means purely quantitative change.   The distinction between 'given resources' and 'resources adapted to demand' is unambiguous only where the adaptation means addition or subtraction.   Where regrouping exists as an alternative mode of change the màtter is no longer quite so simple.   The whole notion is clearly linked to a purely quantitative conception of capital.

For Keynes of course the trade cycle means essentially fluctuations in the degree of utilization of existing resources. The short period is to him the period during which capital under construction emanates the multiplier effect, the long period that in which the new capital begins to produce output. In the Hicksian theory the juxtaposition of autonomous and induced investment amounts to an admission that if we have to explain why there is a ceiling and a bottom we cannot ignore 'long run' factors.

To us the whole division is artificial and unacceptable. Once we realize that industrial fluctuations are not merely a matter of utilizing existing resources in the short run, or increasing and possibly decreasing them in the long run, but also of regrouping them as well as increasing or decreasing them *in certain directions*, the whole *fundamentum divisionis* falls to the ground.

The possibility of multiple use of existing resources in successive periods blurs the simple line of distinction.   This of course does not mean that time does not enter into the problems of capital.   Time is germane to them, but not merely as the dimension in which the 'quantity of Capital' changes, but also as the dimension in which capital resources are turned from one mode of use to another.   It was just for this purpose that in Chapter III we found it necessary to apply a form of period analysis to capital problems.

Moreover, economic progress in the long run also depends

[12] See, for instance, N. Kaldor: 'The Relation of Economic Growth and Cyclical Fluctuations', *Economic Journal*, March 1954.

on the productivity of the new capital which, in its turn, depends on the concrete form of the new resources. This form is determined by investment decisions made 'in the short run', and progress can be hampered by intersectional maladjustment.

In Chapter I (p. 10) we explained that investment opportunities really mean 'gaps' in the existing capital pattern. With respect to progress therefore we may say that the direction of progress depends on where these gaps are, thus using two concepts which would be meaningless in a world of homogeneous capital.

Once the homogeneity hypothesis has been abandoned the distinction between growth and fluctuations loses its meaning. This distinction finds a place in a theory which confines itself to asking whether and to what extent existing resources are being used, whether, and perhaps at what speed, such resources can be augmented, and what are the circumstances in which such augmentation is likely to take place. Once we have learnt to ask how, and in what order, existing resources are being used, and what are the implications of such multiple use, once we have begun to understand the importance of the concrete form of resources in limiting the scope of multiple use, we can easily dispense with the all too simple distinction between economic growth and cyclical fluctuations.

II

Thus far our approach to trade cycle problems has been mainly critical. In examining the Hicksian model we found certain weaknesses. A critical analysis of these provided us with an opportunity to set forth certain ideas which might help us to overcome them. We now have to turn to a more constructive task. The ideas mentioned have to be subjected to a test of coherence by welding them into a model, or at least as much of a model as is necessary to see whether and how they fit together.

The Hicksian theory is a theory of the strong boom. The only other model of the strong boom which has been worked out with any degree of precision is the body of ideas set out originally by Cassel and Spiethoff,[13] and later developed by

[13] Cf. 'Business Cycles', *International Economic Papers*, Vol. 3, pp. 75–171.

Mises[14] and Hayek,[15] which has come to be known as the Austrian Theory of Industrial Fluctuations.[16] Let us see whether with its help we can further develop and apply to the trade cycle the main ideas set forth in this book.

In expounding the Austrian theory there is no need to start *de novo*. It is a body of ideas which has gradually evolved over the last fifty years. But it is necessary first to make some preliminary remarks about its nature, and thus to obviate certain misunderstandings which, experience teaches us, stand in the way of its correct understanding.

In the first place, we do not maintain that the Austrian theory could explain every and any industrial fluctuation that has ever occurred. Such a view of course would be incompatible with our plea for eclecticism. The Austrian theory is a theory of the strong boom, it deals with its causes and consequences. Undoubtedly, weak booms which ended when consumption failed to keep in step with production have occurred in history; America from 1929 to 1932 seems a prominent example. To account for them a different kind of model is required. All we contend here is that an underconsumption theory, which might account for the end of a weak boom, is not exactly a suitable instrument for analysing strong booms. And there is now good historical evidence to show that strong booms were a more or less regular feature of the expanding world economy in its 'normal' conditions from 1870 to 1914.

Secondly, the Austrian theory does not, as is often suggested, assume 'Full Employment'. It assumes that in general, at any moment, some factors are scarce, some abundant. It also assumes that, for certain reasons connected with the production and planned use of capital goods, some of these scarcities become more pronounced during the upswing. Those who criticize the theory on the ground mentioned merely display their inability to grasp the significance of a fundamental fact in the world in which we are living: the heterogeneity of all resources. Unemployment of some factors is not merely compatible with the Austrian theory; unemployment of those

[14] *Human Action*, 1949, Chapter XX.
[15] *Profits, Interest and Investment*, 1939.
[16] See also L. M. Lachmann: 'A Reconsideration of the Austrian Theory of Industrial Fluctuations', *Economica*, May 1940.

factors whose complements cannot come forward in the conditions planned is an essential feature of it.

The Austrian theory does not rest upon a stationary model. Saving and investment play a prominent part in it, while of course in a stationary society there can be no such thing. It is also set against the background of economic expansion. Like Mr. Harrod and Professor Hicks it views industrial fluctuations essentially as deviations from the dynamic equilibrium path of progress. The condition of this dynamic equilibrium path is that planned savings equal planned investment. But the nature of the economic forces which in dynamic equilibrium, i.e. when all plans are consistent with each other, keep the economic system on an even keel by preventing planned investment from either exceeding or falling short of planned saving, and of those counter-forces which in certain circumstances prevent the first set of forces from operating, certainly requires further examination.

Finally, the Austrian theory not merely views industrial fluctuations as the result of maladjustment between planned savings and planned investment, but also as the result of structural maladjustment caused by the first type of maladjustment. In this way it is linked to a dynamic theory of capital of the kind outlined in Chapter V. In economic progress the degree of specialization of resources, in other words the scope there is for multiple use, is linked to the rate of accumulation of capital. Where the latter is misjudged, sooner or later the former will turn out to have been miscalculated.

We said that the conditions of stability in expansion, which keep planned investment within the bounds, and up to the extent, of planned savings, deserve further study. Mrs. Robinson has outlined a model in which these conditions hold and serve to keep the system on an even keel.

When an economy is expanding at the rate appropriate to the given conditions, all prices are equal to long-period average costs (including in cost, profit on capital at the given rate) and all capital equipment is working at the designed capacity. In each sector conditions of rising short-period supply price obtain, so that any increase in output relatively to capacity would be accompanied by a rise in price above long-period average cost.

The capitalists expect the rate of profit to continue in the future to rule at the present level.

Now, if we postulate that the capitalists' expectations of future profits have great inertia and do not react to passing events, the system can be regarded as being in equilibrium from the short-period point of view. A chance increase in consumption would cause the output of consumption goods to rise above designed capacity, prices to rise above normal costs and so profits to rise above their long-run level. But since this state of affairs is not expected to last, investment is not stepped up, and no 'acceleration' occurs. Similarly, a chance increase in investment does not raise expected future receipts (in spite of a rise at the moment, due to the operation of the short-run multiplier). But the prices of capital goods have risen above the normal long-run level, the rate of profit to be expected on funds invested at these prices is less than the accustomed rate, and so, we may suppose, investment is checked. If investment chanced to fall, the price of capital goods would fall, the rate of profit to be expected on funds invested 'at those prices would rise, and investment would pick up again. Thus, the postulate that expectations do not vary with current events may be considered to endow the system with short-period stability, and (combined with faith in future profitability of capital) to provide a presumption that the rate of investment tends to be maintained at a level which continuously corresponds to the gradually growing capacity of the investment-good industries.'[17]

Mrs. Robinson says that she obtained this model by grafting Marshall's analysis on to the Harrodian model. But the reader will not fail to notice how easily the Austrian conception of dynamic equilibrium fits into this mould. To be sure, Mrs. Robinson never mentions savings; to her, as to any Keynesian, savings are of course a mere residual magnitude. But it is obvious that a 'chance increase in consumption' means a fall in planned savings relatively to planned investment; otherwise why should prices rise? And a 'chance increase in investment' which leads to a rise in the prices of capital goods must mean a rise in planned investment relatively to planned saving. The essence of the matter is not merely that 'expectations do not vary with current events', but that prices moving away from their normal and expected level

[17] Joan Robinson: 'The Model of an Expanding Economy', *Economic Journal*, March 1952, pp. 47–8 (by permission of the Royal Economic Society).

provide entrepreneurs with a storm signal; they indicate *ex ante disequilibrium* between savings and investment and tell investors when, and when not, to make new investment decisions. We may add that among these prices and costs rates of interest must play a significant part.

The economic system outlined in this model is kept on an even keel because every deviation from the equilibrium path will, when in an upward direction, release forces which via a rise in costs check investment, and when in a downward direction, stimulate it via a fall in costs. Thus, if the conditions of the model existed in reality, there would be no trade cycle. But at the same time the study of the model has proved worth our while; we now understand better what happens when its conditions are not fulfilled.

Where prices, wages, and rates of interest are inflexible, investment decisions to a large extent have to be made in the dark. Where interest rates are kept constant, no hint of *ex ante* disequilibrium between savings and investment can transpire. Where raw material prices are 'controlled' and no rising wages give a hint of approaching labour shortage, we need not be surprised if we hit the ceiling with full force. The sensitive mechanism which emits the storm signals has been switched off; the deviation of actual prices from their normal and expected level can no longer serve as a measure of disequilibrium and a signpost for action. All this follows simply from what we said in Chapter IV about the role of flexible prices in the sensitive network of communications on which a market economy so largely depends. In such a situation entrepreneurs cannot correctly assess the relative availability and scarcity of the factors to be employed in their investment plans; the impenetrable smoke-screen of a deceptive 'price stability' shrouds them all equally. These plans of course cannot be carried out and disaster is the natural result. Dynamic equilibrium requires consistency of plans which, in its turn, depends on a flexible price system. Inconsistency of plans is an inevitable feature of a world in which prices (including forward prices and share prices) no longer tell an intelligible story.

We now have arrived at a decisive point of our argument. We have seen that in a strong boom entrepreneurs, deluded by factor costs which are not equilibrium costs and therefore can say nothing about available supply, embark on investment projects the resources for which do not exist and cannot be created by a transfer of resources from consumption. Thus far we have not gone beyond what Cassel and Spiethoff said fifty years ago and most economists knew by, say, 1913. At best we have merely explicated the implications of their thesis. The specifically 'Austrian' element, the link with the theory of capital, has now to be brought into our picture. If all capital were homogeneous we should have little more to say about the trade cycle. As it is, the link with the main thesis of this book has now to be forged.

All entrepreneurial decisions are specifying decisions. Investment decisions determine not merely, as Keynes would have it, the 'rate of investment', but also determine the concrete character of each new capital good, whether building, plant, machine, etc. Each new capital good forms part of a whole and has to fit into a capital combination. We pointed out in Chapter III (pp. 49–50) that new investment depends on nothing so much as on the availability of cheap complementary resources of labour and capital. The complementarity of old and new capital goods shows itself within the firm and its production plan, but just as much in the structural overall complementarity of capital resources in the economy. Decisions on the construction of new capital thus involve all these complementarities. The entrepreneur in making his decision will be guided by his expectations about what complementary capital resources will be created during his investment period, and what other already existing resources will then be available in a complementary capacity, in just the same way as he will be guided by expectations about the future supply of labour. A railway is built in the expectation that the economic development of the area served by it will produce enough demand for its services. Engineering industries expand in the expectation that the industries who are their customers will expand at a certain rate. This fact is of some significance for the trade cycle in general and the strong boom in particular.

In Chapter V we learnt that economic progress involves the division of capital along with the division of labour. The more highly developed the economy, the more intricate the degree of

I

complementarity. Thus anything which gives a wrong picture of resources available for investment, and of the speed at which the economy as a whole can expand, will lead to wrong decisions about the degree of specialization of the new capital. That the economy 'hits the ceiling' may mean that a new railway line cannot be completed, or cannot be completed within the time planned, or at the cost planned. But it may also mean that even if it is completed as planned, it will lack complementary factors in the rest of the economy. Such lack of complementary factors may well express itself in a lack of demand for its services, for instance where these factors would occupy 'the later stages of production'. To the untrained observer it is therefore often indistinguishable from 'lack of effective demand'.

Rates of interest which are too low, i.e. fail to establish *ex ante* equilibrium between savings and investment, are apt to convey such a misleading picture and thus to lead to wrong specifying decisions. In the Keynesian world in which idle resources of all kinds are abundant, and are to be had at constant cost in terms of 'wage units', all this does not matter. Here resources can be treated with impunity *as though* they were homogeneous, simply because in any case there are always more than enough of them of whatever category. But in a world in which anything is scarce, and in which construction costs rise with investment demand in a strong boom, all this can hardly be ignored.

The essence of the matter is that investment decisions are not merely irreversible in time, so that excessive investment in period 1 as a rule cannot be offset by disinvestment in period 2, but that they are also irrevocable in kind. Even if, at a later point during the boom, interest rates start to rise, the message comes too late for those who have made their irrevocable decision before. If all capital were homogeneous there would be no sub-ceilings and the advance would not be halted until all resources had become equally scarce—Keynes' point of full employment and full utilization. As it is, capital is heterogeneous, and the first sub-ceiling reached will necessitate not merely the revision of plans for the construction of new capital, but also the revision of plans for the use of existing capital.

III

We now turn to our last task in this chapter: to survey the problems which emerge on the morrow of the crisis, and to study ways and means by which they might be solved. The reader, we trust, will not expect to be told of an 'adjustment mechanism'; in the realm of human action there is no such thing. A market economy, to be sure, has great resilience and can adapt itself to many needs, sudden as well as long foreseen. But this is not because of any automatic mechanism 'built-in' but because it serves in general to put the right man on the right spot. Successful adjustment to new conditions no less than whatever 'stable progress' there might exist, depend ulti- mately on the entrepreneurial qualities of mind and will which manifest themselves in response to challenge. Situations like those we shall study provide a crucial test of entrepreneurial ability.

We may remind the reader that we are primarily dealing with the situation which arises when a strong boom has col- lapsed as a result of the encounter with a ceiling, or at least a sufficiently tough congeries of sub-ceilings. This does not mean, however, that the situation which follows the end of a weak boom is none of our concern. It is of interest to us to the extent to which it gives rise to the need for capital re- grouping; this need it shares with the aftermath of a strong boom. But this is not to say that capital regrouping by itself will suffice to overcome the situation following the end of a weak boom. As a rule it will not, and there may be much scope for the Keynesian nostrums. No doubt such an under- consumption crisis, due to a flagging 'effective demand', can be at least mitigated by increasing this demand, though it must remain a matter for decision in each case whether its investment or its consumption component needs to be strength- ened. The need for capital regrouping arises from the peculiar characteristics of these circumstances.

Another point calls for notice: Any sudden and unexpected change in the 'real situation' will probably affect the demand for and the velocity of circulation of money. In the case under discussion widespread disappointment with the results of the past, the need for plan revision, the general loss of confidence, will almost certainly have this effect. In a monetary system based on bank deposits, i.e. debts, in which the mere maintenance of any given quantity of money requires continuous agreement between creditors and debtors, the quantity of money can hardly remain unaffected. In particular, where the banks are involved in some of the investment schemes which have gone astray, the danger of *secondary deflation* is always present. When that happens the 'recession' which succeeded the strong boom will turn into a 'depression', a cumulative process of income contraction, as has often happened in the past. Of course it need not happen. But to avert the danger must always be the primary aim of monetary policy in a recession. The reader is asked always to bear this in mind in the discussion which follows.

We now turn to the main issue. The situation which the economy faces on the morrow of the collapse of a strong boom clearly calls for capital regrouping on a large scale. On this score the reader who has followed the main line of thought of this book will have no doubt. The questions which arise are rather, what form the regrouping shall take and what are the circumstances favourable or detrimental to it. Plans have gone astray, hopes have been disappointed; capital combinations have to be dissolved and reshuffled. But what is the principle governing these changes?

Some planned combinations cannot come into operation because of lack of complementary factors; these factors have to be created now. But in general the rate of expansion of the whole economy will have to slow down. Yet the situation we confront is not, like that of a war or post-war economy, one of universal shortage. The scarcities are relative only. Something might be done by shifting resources to where they are most needed. The critical sectors are those sub-ceilings which lie in the path of expansion. Here more investment is required in order to 'lift the ceiling'. To this end not merely must investment in other sectors be curtailed; additional factors able to help in lifting the ceiling must be recruited from wherever they happen to be, and this means as a rule that they must be withdrawn from those combinations of which they form part. Mobile resources from everywhere, even from the consumption goods industries, will have to be drawn to the critical sectors.

All this plays no part in the Hicksian theory. For Professor Hicks the slope of the ceiling in general, and the configuration of critical sub-ceilings in particular, are the long-run product of autonomous investment, something that lies entirely beyond the grasp of short-run action. It is true of course that this configuration of sub-ceilings is, at each moment, the cumulative result of forces that have operated in the past, but it does not follow that therefore nothing can be done about it in the short run. To us it is impossible, for the reasons mentioned, to separate the forces of progress from those of the cycle. To us the configuration of particular sub-ceilings is something that can be re-moulded by changing its composition, though it might be unwise to expect early results to transform the situation entirely.

In general the chief remedy for recession lies in increased investment in the critical sectors, even where such investment does not yield early results, and in the concomitant withdrawal of mobile resources from existing combinations. These mobile resources have to be detached from the specific and non-mobile resources with which so far they have co-operated, and this will lead to dissolution and reshuffling of existing combinations.

Such action creates a number of practical problems. The owners of the mobile resources of course act under the stimulus of the high earnings obtainable at their place of destination, but the owners of the specific resources to which until yesterday the mobile resources were complements, may have good reason to mourn their departure. Even where these mobile resources are not irreplaceable the earnings of specific factors are certain to be reduced.

The owners of a factory are unlikely to close it and let their plant lie idle merely because their liquid capital could earn a higher rate of interest elsewhere. But here the control structure is of some importance. In certain cases the creditors may compel their reluctant debtors to part with their mobile assets. In general we may say that where the division between the firm's own capital and its debts corresponds most closely to that between its first-line, and its second-line and reserve assets, i.e. its fixed and mobile resources, the chances of successful withdrawal of the mobile resources are highest, precisely because all the gain will accrue to the creditors and all the loss to the debtors. While, where the creditors own also part of the fixed first-line assets, they may be reluctant to incur the capital loss here involved. But in any case there will be enough resistance to all attempts to mobilize resources and disintegrate existing combinations to make the withdrawal of mobile factors a slow and precarious business.

This creates a problem for monetary policy. In all probability mobile resources cannot be withdrawn and capital combinations will not be reshuffled without pressure being brought to bear on owners and managers of specific resources. In some cases it may not be possible at all without actual bankruptcy. To this end a 'severe' credit policy is required. But a credit policy sufficiently severe to 'crack open' the tougher kind of unsuccessful capital combinations may discourage investment in the critical sectors of the economy.

Clearly this is a problem of policy which does not admit of a general answer. In such a situation there is much to be said for a 'selective' credit policy which need not be arbitrary if it merely reflects the degree of imperfection of the capital market which is the natural product of the past record of success and failure of individual firms.[18]

The problem of surmounting intersectional maladjustment must not, however, be viewed exclusively as falling within the narrow context of the firm and its internal complementarities. We saw in Chapter IV that the same capital may give rise to service streams of very different kinds. An industrial economy has often a high degree of flexibility which may operate without much visible disintegration of combinations. Often the change is brought about by using the same plant to produce different products. Suppose our critical sub-ceiling is in mineral mining. It is surely unnecessary to deprive existing coal mines of their mining equipment. Our purpose of moving mobile resources to the critical area may be as well served by the heavy engineering industries switching their plants from pro-

[18] While this is hardly the place to discuss the imperfection of the capital market in general, it must be clear, from what was said in the previous chapter about the interrelationship between plan structure and portfolio structure, that the willingness of the capital market to lend to, or acquire shares in, individual enterprises will to some extent depend on their past record. The degree of imperfection of the capital market is thus largely *not a datum but a result of the market process.*

ducing equipment for coal-using industries to producing mining (or 'mineral-economizing') machinery. In this way existing combinations may be moved bodily to 'another stage of production' without the painful need for disintegration. In such cases internal complementarity is preserved at the expense of structural complementarity. The complementarity relationship which hitherto linked the engineering industries to their customers in the consumer goods trades, the complementarity between successive stages of production, will now be broken; it is impossible to have change and to maintain all existing relationships of complementarity. Those changes which are necessary to rectify the inconsistent capital changes of the boom must not be expected to leave incomes and asset values intact.[19]

It follows that any policy designed merely to restore the *status quo* in terms of 'macro-economic' aggregate magnitudes, such as incomes and employment, is bound to fail. The state prior to the downturn was based on plans which have failed; hence a policy calculated to discourage entrepreneurs from revising their plans, but to make them 'go ahead' with the same capital combinations as before, cannot succeed. Even if business men listen to such counsel they would simply repeat their former experience. What is needed is a policy which promotes the necessary readjustments. No doubt, if the actual break-up of existing combinations with its consequences for control structure and portfolio structure can be avoided, readjustment will be much easier, but it is clearly impossible to maintain all those asset values which were based on inconsistent plans. What happens during a strong boom is that resources are being given a concrete form which, but for the misguided expectations of the boom, would not have been chosen. Somebody has to take the consequences.

We saw that even where the breaking-up of existing firms can be avoided, there will nevertheless have to be a break in structural complementarity. It follows that a policy endeavouring merely to 'maintain effective demand' by stimulating

[19] 'One must provide the capital goods lacking in those branches which were unduly neglected in the boom. Wage rates must drop; people must restrict their consumption temporarily until the capital wasted by malinvestment is restored. Those who dislike these hardships of the readjustment period must abstain in time from credit expansion'—L. von Mises: *Human Action*, pp. 575–6.

consumption will simply defeat the very purpose of readjustment by making it profitable for those who should deflect the flow of their services elsewhere, to let them flow where they did before.

Thus far in this chapter we have been concerned with the strong boom. The strong boom is the result of plans involving inconsistent capital change, and this inconsistency is the result of the fact that where prices are inflexible they convey misleading information about available resources. As it is clearly impossible to have completely flexible prices in reality, or even an equal degree of flexibility throughout the economic system, investment decisions based on erroneous assumptions about the future availability of resources cannot easily be avoided. Even if all prices were completely flexible and sensitive to all present changes in demand and supply they would, in the absence of a fairly comprehensive system of forward markets which would make all relevant expectations consistent with each other, not necessarily reflect future scarcity of resources. Those who have to make investment plans might still be misled about the future availability of the resources they need if they relied exclusively on these present prices. The strong boom is thus an almost inevitable concomitant of an expanding industrial economy, and the system-wide regrouping of capital is its necessary consequence and corrective.

This does not mean that nothing can be done to mitigate it. There is one price in particular which, owing to its strategic importance, we should attempt to make as flexible as possible: the rate of interest, the general rate of exchange between present and future goods. When present goods are withdrawn from immediate use and turned into sources of future output, i.e. in the later stages of a strong boom, the rate of interest should rise. Any attempt to prevent it from rising means to spread misleading information about present and impending scarcities and future abundance. This is clearly seen on the Stock Exchange which discounts future yield streams on the basis of the present rate of interest. A sensitive and well-informed market witnessing the spectacle of a strong boom will of course in any case sooner or later have its misgivings about future yields and the cost of present projects. But we need not doubt that where this is not so, a rising rate of interest would strongly reinforce the discounting factor and thus damp excessive optimisim.

Capital regrouping is thus the necessary corrective for the maladjustment engendered by a strong boom, but its scope is not confined to this kind of maladjustment. Where a weak boom has 'petered out' before 'hitting the ceiling' capital regrouping is just as necessary. That this is not at once obvious is due to the unfortunate habit of viewing all these problems in 'macro-economic' terms. If we come to believe that the only reason why expansion suffers a check is the combination of a weak accelerator with a feeble multiplier, we shall of course conclude that the only proper remedy is an increase in effective demand, and that it does not really matter how this is accomplished.

Even in a weak boom, however, some industries expand more than others, new products come into the market, consumers change their preferences, and in general, with or without full employment, some factors are scarcer than others. The new capital combinations will change the capital structure and the new products modify the market structure. Here again price inflexibility will for a time tend to hide the facts from the entrepreneurs, but the inconsistencies will show themselves in the end. This situation is best viewed in terms of Schumpeter's model in which the 'innovating' new firms expand into 'new economic space' but also restrict the range of action of the older firms. As a result the latter have to adjust themselves to the new conditions, and this entails capital regrouping.

At the end of a weak boom the new capital resources begin to pour out output. Here there is no difficulty in obtaining and keeping together the complementary factor combinations since the ceiling has not been hit. But some firms may find it difficult to dispose of the new output. Prices will tend to fall, employment may decline and unsold stocks accumulate. Excess capacity (of the 'real kind'!) may make its appearance. The notion that in such a case we could simply restore the *status quo* by 'maintaining incomes' is, however, here just as futile as in the case of the recession following the strong boom. It is true of course that there is a danger that such an underconsumption crisis may degenerate into a cumulative depression. If so, a budget deficit may help. But such a policy would have to be supplemented by strong pressure for the necessary capital regrouping to take place. Attempts, which are very likely in such situations, to 'stabilize' prices will, by reducing consumers' real incomes, simply make adjustment more difficult. The best remedy for the excess capacity mentioned is to make it unprofitable for the owners of such resources to maintain them. Except in the case where there is excess capacity everywhere, the case in the contemplation of which the Keynesians specialize, existing capital combinations must be broken up and their fragments removed to wherever they are still useful. As in the case of the aftermath of the strong boom, a selective credit policy which reflects the degree of imperfection of the capital market, appears to be called for.

The significance of capital regrouping thus transcends the phenomena of the strong boom. But it also transcends the Austrian Theory of Industrial Fluctuations and its logical basis, the theory of capital we expounded in Chapter V. The Austrian theory, as most other models except Schumpeter's, ignores the effects of innovation and technical progress. It views economic progress primarily as taking place along the lines of ever greater division of labour and specialization of capital equipment, of ever higher degrees of complexity of factor combinations. But technical progress may cancel some of these effects by making some specialized skills and other specific characteristics redundant. 'Technological Unemployment' of highly skilled craftsmen is of course a well-known manifestation of this tendency. Technical progress, however, while making some capital equipment redundant, raises the demand for other types and their complements. All this simply means that in a world in which the forces of progress are manifold there are more, and not fewer, forces abroad which make the regrouping of capital an ineluctable task.

Technical progress means unexpected change. It is by no means the only form of unexpected change which entails modifications of the capital structure. In reality the capital structure is ever changing. Every day the network of plans is torn, every day it is mended anew. Plans have to be revised, new capital combinations are formed, and old combinations disintegrate. Without the often painful pressure of the forces of change there would be no progress in the economy; without the steady action of the entrepreneurs in specifying the uses of capital and modifying such decisions, as the forces of change unfold, a civilized economy could not survive at all.

INDEX

Acceleration coefficient, 103–4
Assets, 87–99
Austrian Theory of Industrial Fluctuations, 113 et seq., 126

Boehm-Bawerk, E. v., v, 11, 73, 78 et seq.
Boulding, K. E., 88n

Capital
— accumulation (*see* Investment)
— coefficients, 42, 80
— complementarity, 3, 12, 54, 80, 85, 108, 117–18, 121–2
— definition of, 11–12
— division of, 79 et seq., 103, 118
— gains and losses, 17–18, 37–8, 94–5
— heterogeneity of, 2, 12, 73, 118
— regrouping, 35 et seq., 48, 51, 58, 93, 97, 119–27
— structure, 4, 7, 10, 12, 53, 57–60, 72, 80
— supplementary, 42, 90
Cassel, G., 17, 79, 112, 117
Control structure, 91, 121, 123

Duesenberry, J. S., 105

Eastham, J. K., 68n
Economic progress, 17–19, 37, 79–85, 103, 126
Entrepreneur, 16–17, 97–9
Equilibrium analysis, 39, 46–8
Equilibrium, dynamic, 60, 114–16
Excess capacity, 49, 52, 109, 125
Expectations, 8, 15, 20–34, 115–17

Factor complementarity, and substitution, 56
Fisher, I., 11
Forward markets, 67, 76
Frankel, S. H., 11n, 18n
'Functionless' price movements, 24, 33, 62–3, 65

Harrod, R. F., 17, 58, 79, 102
Hawtrey, R. G., 64n

Hayek, F. A., viii, 2n, 12, 52, 54n, 60, 77, 113
Hicks, J. R., 17, 39, 55, 58, 68n, 79, 100 et seq.

Interest, rate of, 7, 74–8, 118, 124
Investment (*ees also* Malinvestment), 6–7, 10, 37, 49, 52, 79, 96, 114 et seq., 120
— autonomous and induced, 103, 108–10

Kaldor, N., 64n, 111n
Keynes, Lord, 6, 10, 50, 68–71, 75n, 77, 111, 118, 119
Knight, F. H., v, 26n, 83

Lachmann, L. M., 26, 32n, 57n, 113n
Lange, O., 25, 30, 65
Lerner, A. P., 6, 75n, 81
Lewis, W. A., 105–6
Lindahl, E., 13–14, 39, 74, 78
Liquidity preference, 51–2, 88–9
Lundberg, E., 39, 104

Makower, H., 88n
Malinvestment, 17, 25, 37, 66
Market process, 28–9
Marschak, J., 88n
Menger, C., 54n
Mises, L. v., 26n, 55, 113, 123n

Neisser, H., 47

Palander, T., 50n
Plan complementarity, 54
Plan structure, 54, 91
Portfolio structure, 55, 91, 123
Price inflexibility, 29, 63 et seq., 77, 116
Price system, 21–2, 62 et seq.
Process analysis, 13–15, 39 et seq.
Production plans, 10, 13, 35 et seq., 54

Range, inner and outer, 30–4
Reserve assets, 90, 92, 95
Robinson, J., 6, 49, 69n, 114–15

129

Schumpeter, J. A., 125-6
Scitovszky, T. de, 63
Securities, 90 et seq.
Shackle, G. L. S., 26-9
Specificity, multiple, 2, 12
Spiethoff, A., 112, 117
Sraffa, P., 76-7
Stock Exchange, 67-71
Streeten, P., 63
Structural complementarity, 54, 109, 117, 122-3
Structural maladjustments, 59, 60, 108, 114
Sweezy, P. M., 63

Technical progress, 79, 103, 126
Terborgh, G., 38
Time (as a measure of capital), 73, 83-5

Underdeveloped areas, 18-19
Uthwatt Committee, 28-9

Vertical disintegration, 83

Wages Fund, 5
Walras, L., 11
Wholesale trade, 64
Wicksell, K., v, 2n, 77